# Don't Talk About IT, Be About IT

## AN AUTOBIOGRAPHY OF MALIK

**MALIK**

ISBN:  978-1-64314-437-5 (Paperback)
       978-1-64314-438-2 (Hardback)

AuthorsPress
California, USA
www.authorspress.com

# Acknowledgments

I want to thank God first and foremost. Thanks also to my mom, my kids, and my brothers and sister. Thanks to Grandmother, Granddaddy, and my aunts, uncles, cousins, and my babies' mothers. Thanks to my whole family and friends, pastors, church members, classmates, and all of my wonderful friends who stayed with me through the good and bad times. Thanks to my wonderful friends at my publishing company. I thank everyone for the support. If I forgot anyone, you are special in my life also. I love you.

# Table of Contents

# Introduction

When I first began contemplating compiling facts, figures, and experiences of my life, the first thing that came to my mind was how I was going to facilitate an accurate order. Then I wondered what it was about me that I thought was of value to add to the wide body of public knowledge. Third, who would be my reading audience, and last, was there a real market for autobiographies of the life and works of an African American southerner who just wanted to share? After all, I am not making any attempt to compare myself or my contributions to that of Saint Augustine of Hippo, who wrote about his life around the fourth century. In his writings, he regrets so many things, including his belief in astrology, his sexual sins, and being part of the Manichaean religion. Nevertheless, Saint Augustine was a great man, and I urge the reader to continue to read and respect his contributions.

Unlike Saint Augustine, I do not regret the past, because the past is over and will not come again. I am, however, mindful of the past so that the unpleasant things that I have done, both knowingly and out of mere ignorance, will not be repeated.

In this work, I would like to state the truth and how I was able to confront and overcome some obstacles. I would like to share experiences that I feel young people, regardless of race, religion, or orientation, can use in their own personal growth. Some aspects of my life have not been so good, but other parts of it display how I have evolved in our money-driven and ever-changing society.

The primary purpose of this book is to share the feelings of my life, my philosophy, and the outcomes of my journey on earth. It has been a short journey but nevertheless a lesson well earned.

# I. The Formative Years

As a young kid growing up in the projects in a small town, life was a challenge. My mom was able to raise four sons and a daughter. It was tough but a noble experience for my mom, who had an accurate understanding of family, love, patience, and struggle. These qualities were necessary for her survival as well as the survival of the children. Deserting the family or going crazy was not an option for Mom, because she had kids to rise. She always said that boys were much harder to raise than her girl. After all, she wanted her boys to grow up to be responsible and God-fearing men.

My mom would walk ten miles to work and back to make sure we had food on the table. My mom was a true woman of God and never went out to party or hang out with her friends. I can remember that every Wednesday night, we would have to attend Bible study in order to get the knowledge to be grounded when we became adults. Then on Sundays, we went to church to listen to the good word from the preacher.

I always considered Mom to be a strong black woman who was very humble and understanding. She had to have been, because she made it through the struggle of Jim Crow in the South and was able to maintain cohesiveness in our family structure. Jim Crow was a blatant racial caste system in Southern and border states. It started during the latter part of the 1800s and came to a peak in the 1960s. This system brought about anti-black laws. With all of this going on, my mom persevered and never held hatred in her heart for anyone.

Also, I had a stepdad who really cared about me becoming a successful young man. I never met my real dad. My stepdad loved and enjoyed cookouts with family and friends.

The projects was a housing development where we shared many good memories and great ideas as to how to improve it for the betterment of those who lived there. There were people there who worked, and there were others who were constantly searching for employment.

There were times that my mom found it difficult to purchase affordable clothing for us. Of course, this was understandable because she was raising so many children on a fixed income. This prompted my brother Johnny, who was fourteen, to take me, at age eight, with him to earn money cutting grass on the outskirts of our community. My oldest brother had that entrepreneurial spirit at a young age. He also knew his duty and loyalty to the family as the eldest son. My five-year-old brother often tagged along; he would help carry the gas container, and once in a while, we would let him cut a little bit. My younger sister, over whom all of us were probably overprotective, would almost always stay home to comfort my mom. In so many ways, my sister and mother were very close. My youngest brother loved to watch television, so he did not get the chance to work as an infant.

When I did not work, I would go to the cookie store and get two windmill cookies for a penny a piece. Then I'd get all my friends together, and we would play baseball all day until the street lights came on. Baseball was something we did together so that we would not get in trouble. It was an enjoyable athletic sport that was low maintenance; after all, one only needed a bat or stick on a wide field. There were numerous empty fields around in those days, and we played the game until we dropped. However, as soon as the street lights turned on, we were off the field because all of us had to be in the house. There was no exception to the rule unless my mom was sending me to the fish store to get a couple of fish sandwiches for the family.

Most people that I knew in the housing development were often going in and out of juvenile detention. It was amazing because the petty things that many of them were involved in did not really warrant that type of reprimand. This is not to say that there were not others who actually deserved jail time. I was always saddened when a few of my friends had to go into youth detention. I had a very strict mom, and there were behavior patterns that were unacceptable to her. My friends always stayed positive and looked after one another. My friend Pablo would look after me if someone attempted to beat me up. He was the best fighter in the neighborhood. Everyone misjudged him, but he had a good heart. My cousin Terry would tell Pablo to look after me; they were best friends. It was a challenge to grow up with these guys.

When we were not playing baseball, we would walk to the university to see football or baseball games. We really loved sports. At a young age, we had a dream to become professional players when we grew up. Coaches and staff saw us all the time, so they would let us get in the game some. My friend D-Nice was closest to me, and we would go to his house to play games and help his mom around the house while she prepared dinner. His mom considered me as a son, especially after she knew everything that was going on with my family issues D-Nice had a cousin named Peter who would watch me play baseball in the front yard, and he would say, "One day you are going to be a superstar." I didn't know what he was saying at first until he explained everything to me.

We had some next door neighbors who were usually nice guys, but they loved to fight all the time. I can remember going to the store for my mom to get something to cook for dinner. Two of the guys next door bullied me to give them my mom's change from the groceries. My mom humbly replied, "Don't worry, baby, God will deal with them one day." She always believed God could do anything if one believed with faith the size of a mustard seed.

At the age of nine, I became more focused and got deeper into school work and baseball. At a young age I was determined to become a star. Peter would come by my house and ask me if I would like to come to one of his baseball games so that I could get an idea why I loved the game so much. This was the first time I got to really see a different side of life, instead of the projects all the time. I used to go play basketball at the gym, and the teachers Mr. Tom and Tepee showed me discipline.

I enjoyed the game. The score was close, and Axel won by two in the final innings. After the game he introduced me to his coach and team and announced, "This is going to be the next superstar in little league in the future." I replied that he was just joking. The whole season I would go to his practices and participate with the team. My coach, Eric, took me under his wings and guided me to be the best. He would pick me up and take me home for practices.

This was a great experience for me. My mom wanted me to stop going to practice with Peter because she wanted me to help my grandmother for the rest of the summer. When I got out of school, I went to Grandmom's house, where she was really strict about everything. When I would get in trouble with my cousin, who stayed with my grandmother at the time, she'd tell us to go outside and get the biggest switch on a tree. She would beat us with no pants on, just skin. My grandmom taught me a lot about the Bible and how to humble myself in bad situations. My cousin and I would go to the store for her so that she could make great home-cooked meals. I'm hungry right now thinking about it. We would clean the house well so that in the morning she could cook her amazing cheese biscuits. The cheese biscuits would have cheese dripping from the bread.

My grandmom and aunt were the foundation for keeping the extended family together. Every Thanksgiving and Christmas, all the family members would get together to enjoy the celebration. My aunt cooked the best fish in the world. When the elder people gathered in the living room to talk about different issues, we kids were not allowed to come near the living room. My aunt would leave a couple of fish in the fryer to cool down until dinner, and I would sneak in the kitchen and grab a couple of pieces. I loved fish so much that they gave me the nickname Fish.

My other aunt and cousin would come down from their hometown every year. The whole family, in the state and out of state, would get together to play music and enjoy each other. I loved visiting my cousins Melvin and Derrick, and their mom and dad would stop to enjoy the fun and games we put together. Their dad loved playing horseshoes, and they would always have something good on the grill. They knew how to have a good time. Most of my family loved the Lord, so we would have church right at the house. When the celebration was over, my cousin and I would clean up and get ready for a two-on-two basketball game in the back yard. My family loved sports, especially my uncles, because they would bet money on every game. If I wasn't playing baseball that summer,

I would stay with my grandmom the whole summer, and she would put us to work around the house with different assignments.

I remember we had to go to work with my uncle Paul in the potato field, where it was 150 degrees. He would work from 7:00 AM to 6:00 PM. I helped for about a month, just to make enough money to buy some school clothes. My uncle was real cool and always tried to find a way to make a dollar. He had to, because he produced so many kids. He had eleven children and took care of each and every one of them. As my uncle Paul was taking us back to my grandmother's house, he explained the value of life. "If you have kids, they are the first priority to you." I took it in very deeply because I knew one day I was going to have some beautiful kids of my own.

We arrived at Grandmother's house, and the first thing she said was, "Take a shower and get ready for bed," because we had to read a scripture in the Bible before we went to bed. My cousins always took care of my grandmother, even when she got sick on different occasions.

For the rest of the summer, I needed to make money because school was right around the corner. I asked my grandmother whether I could go to work with my uncle picking tobacco or something. I did that for about a month and a half.

I did pretty well for the summer, and now it was time to go school shopping and go home to Mom. My first day in school was perfect, and I made new friends right away. Of course, there always was a bully in every school, and I met this guy named Carl, who was older than me. One day I was walking home, and he kept popping me on my head. I ran home and told my stepdad. He stated that if I didn't go back out there and kick his butt, I would not get back in the house. I beat Carl like I owned him.

The rest of the school year went by very smoothly, until I met this girl named Precious who lived behind my mom's house. I wanted to speak to her, but I was shy at the time. One afternoon the guys and I decided to play hide and seek around the house, and we asked Precious and her sister if they would like to join us. They replied, "We would love to." I kept my eye on Precious the whole time as my friend started the countdown. When she went and hid behind my brother, I was right behind her. I wanted to talk to her alone herself. We finally had a conversation, and she said, "I like you, too. Can we be friends?" We became friends for a long time.

The projects always had a lot of challenges for kids without a lot of money. We would play football in a huge field with the whole neighborhood. This was where I obtained my talents to become a superstar in high school. The boys next door made me tough on the field, and I learned how to become a real man at a young age. When you don't have a father figure, you have to turn to whatever makes you happy inside. Some guys turned to selling drugs and having money and women. I remember everyone following the biggest drug dealer in the whole town. Sweet Dee and Smoky would ride through my neighborhood with a black Samurai Sunki with a loud system playing "Ain't no half steppin'." This was in the early eighties. I loved the fame because it brought the women to the yard.

My goals were to become good in sports and get my mom out of the neighborhood, because she worked hard to make sure we had a roof over our heads. I would practice day in and day out with the boys next door, going over different moves. They saw something in me to be the best in the future. My cousin Jake would pick me up and take me away from the temptation, which was easy to get involved in though word of mouth. My cousins and friends would come to the house to see if we wanted to play football every day. I remember one day my brother was having a good game, and then all of a sudden one of the next-door guys, Tim, hit my brother so hard he went straight into a ditch and stayed there for a while. We talked about that for years, because he was so muddy on him when he got out of the ditch. We always had conflicts in the neighborhood, but we still played basketball at the gym every Saturday almost all day. Pablo would get a fight started by throwing anybody's brand-new shoes on top of the gym. There weren't too many people who would start a fight with him. It was the good day because everyone would get together later, meet under the street lights, and talk about everything that happened in the neighborhood. I would ride my bike to the Trade Mart to get some good cheese biscuits from Ms.

Belinda, who cooked the best biscuits in town. I loved to see her because she would always encourage me to do better in life.

# II. My Relationship with My Family

My cousins interacted with my mom and family every weekend. My aunt stated one day to my mom, "They remember having fun and coming to your house to play with your boys' friends in the neighborhood water fights."

My brother next to me and my cousin from out of town were about the same age, but my younger cousin always hung with me. I noticed we had a connection with sports that made our bond strong. He was the youngest, tagging along with us to the baseball stadium or to the gym to play basketball. My cousin's childhood was great. Every time he came to my hometown, it felt like Christmas to him. I really loved when all of us went to my grandmother's house to play basketball. We would play two on two when my cousin stayed with my grandmother, and I played against my older brother and my cousin all day long. My oldest brother always came to all my baseball games to run the baseball down every time I would hit a homerun. He and my cousin Tom would hold a deep conversation about life during the baseball game. Everybody at the park knew about my brother because he was the first to come to all my games. My brother always kept me focused on life to improve my game plan. Every time he would go to do a job cutting grass, he would take me so that I could learn how to be independent. My brother got his license at the age of seventeen, and that inspired me to stay focused on that. He bought his first car, a brown Camaro with a loud system in the trunk. At night he would ride though Sports World, a skating rink, to impress the people standing on the sidewalk. I remember at Sports World there would always be a showdown to see who was the best rapper around the world. They would battle, rapping on the microphone throughout the night. Sports World was the place to enjoy playing different video games and to get your skating skills up for the competition every Sunday.

My brother next to me was very impressive when he started preaching at the age of twelve, which encouraged a lot of young people to get closer to God. I remember going to church to visit on his preaching days; most of the people in the church enjoyed the service. He is a righteous and intelligent brother, and he is well grounded because of my precious mom. He always began a scripture and would study it to complete the service. My sister always stayed to herself, learning a lot from my mom. She learned the rules of the house and how to cook well. She had a couple of friends to come visit her, but she said she had one best friend, Evelyn. I dated Evelyn's sister Tomeka while growing up. Most of the positive things that my sister learned came from my mom. My sister is very successful now because of being grounded. She is truly a woman of God, like my mom.

My youngest brother has a story more like mine. He went through a lot but is now successful. He loves to do a lot of electrical work. He married a lovely lady and had beautiful kids, which kept him grounded. My brother and his family always get together with us for cookouts.

My uncles did the grilling and talked about everything they'd done in their pasts. My aunts would gather around and talk about the words of the Lord. We would always go to my Aunt Paula's, my mom's aunt, to have a good time and sample all of her cakes. My granddaddy would always take us fishing in order to learn the peaceful life. My granddaddy was very humble and loved to play his music every Sunday. He loved to play the guitar at different churches on the east coast. His wife was pretty cool at times, but no one is perfect. He would show me how to take parts off old cars and assemble them into new parts. He loved to tend to turtles and snails, and he had a lot of them.

I never knew who my real daddy was, so I could not get to know that side of the family. It upset me sometimes, but it could only make me stronger. I finally got information on him, but I'd heard he had died. I was okay with it because my father was in heaven. That was what saw me through the storm.

I love my family because they know how to have a good time. My family is very spiritual and is willing to help anyone in need.

I had a lot of fun with my cousins Tim, Daniel, and Wallace. I remember when I was getting into a lot of trouble, my cousin, who stayed near the projects, would tell me to get off of the streets and get myself together before it was too late to be successful. She really loved me a lot. I thanked her every day for caring for my soul. When she would leave me and I thought I was free, my cousin would come around the corner and say, "I am watching you, and I will tell Grandmom and Granddad." I loved her for that because she cared about my well-being.

When my cousin and I would get together and go to the cookouts and university football events, I had to sell most of my drugs around the corner while peeping at my cousin. We would have cookouts every day to keep the neighbors together. My favorite cousin would have a block party for the whole neighborhood. People would get together and talk about everything that was going on in the town, and they'd eat and drink until they were stuffed. My cousin in a wheelchair would act crazy when he got drunk. He would do tricks in the wheelchair and try to race every car on the highway. My cousin De-Loo would have to save him from doing a lot of crazy things to himself. When my cousin in the wheelchair came into some money from an accident, he went out and bought everything in the town. He bought some gold rims for his wheelchair, with a loud system on the side.

The family always enjoyed the goodness of God when they prayed for something. I would stay at Grandma's house on my stepdad's side when my mom was at work. We had fun swinging on different trees and getting lost in the woods. My cousins Doc and Steve were playing the field with the women. We would go watch the girls in the Moyewood neighborhood, who played jumping jacks and hopscotch all day long.

My uncle Henry Jr. would get drunk and start praising the Lord throughout the whole neighborhood, to let everyone know the goodness of the Lord. He used to try to get all the kids together and tell us about having something when we got older, and he'd tell us not to drink. He was telling us this when he was so drunk he was falling down, and still he was trying to explain the importance of life.

My stepdad's sisters and the twins always stuck together as I was growing up. My grandma would cook some good jiffy cornbread, beans, and barbeque ribs. Every family reunion would be packed, and Henry Jr. would do his part again to let everyone know he was there. I have a wonderful family, and everyone was grounded with the Lord.

# III. My Athletic Years

My athletic career started as the backup quarterback for my junior high school in the eighth grade. It was a great challenge for me at a young age. I was nervous because the ninth-grade team had some big guys, especially Bobby. I would go to the line and look for him. We would practice all day in the summer until school started again. I remember the coach would say, "Go to church Sunday, pay your 10 percent to God, and eat a collard sandwich to get healthier."

The older guys would show me different tricks to becoming a great football player at a young age. I remember my coaches let me start with the first team to get better, because they knew I had a great arm to get the ball down the field. One day I called a play to pass the ball down field, and somebody forgot to block Darryl during the process. He hit me so hard that my whole body was stuck to the ground. My team members had to help me get out the pads, because they were embedded in the grass. We had a great season, a 10-0 record.

The year finally arrived when I was the starting quarterback in ninth grade. I remember roughing up one of my big players in the hallway of southwest middle school.. It made him tougher because he started every game at southwest middle school.. I watched a lot of college football to get the options and passes down completely, so that I could become one the best ever coming out of southwest middle school.. I was very good, especially handing the ball off to a superstar named Anthony Thompson. He became one of the best running backs at the high school level. My arm was so good that one of my passes knocked James Boldwin's shoulder pads off his shoulders. My favorite receiver was Mike Williams; we could connect an eighty-yard pass anytime we wanted. God blessed me with a golden arm at a young age. Anthony Thompson was so well-known that the high school coaches would come out to see him every game. They didn't know they were in for a surprise to see a golden arm from a fifteen-year-old boy throwing the ball seventy yards in the air. I was fast and could throw the ball on the run during the game. After the game, the high school coaches would come up to me and say that in the future, I would be their quarterback in high school. We had a wonderful season, ending with a 9-1 record. That year I dated the hottest cheerleader, Ashley. We had a wonderful relationship—until she decided to date my cousin.

I also played basketball, and I would score about twenty points a game. The best player on the team was Gerald, and at that time he reminded me of a superstar in the NBA. I started dating a girl name Tina Wallace during basketball season. She loved basketball and would come to all of the games with her popcorn and drink. Tina Wallace and I broke up after the basketball season. During basketball season we would have pep rallies for all of the athletes throughout the season.

After basketball season it was time to get ready for my favorite sport, baseball. I had been playing baseball since I was eleven years old. I started playing catcher and pitcher for the team. I was a good hitter, with an average of .400 the whole season. I played with the same crew from little league, so we understood each other's moves on the field. During the baseball season I meet this girl name Shelia Hendricks, and we started dating. She had just moved here from out of state. We had a great season and went undefeated.

In the summer I started baseball season playing catcher and pitcher for a well-known organization. I was hitting homeruns four hundred feet—at the age of fifteen. God really gave me a talent. My experience playing with an older crowd of players made me mature quickly so that I could get ready for the American Legion league. I spent all of my time at baseball fields so that I wouldn't get into trouble on the streets. My old little league baseball coach came to my house one day to give me some advice about playing in American Legion ball, where pro scouts came to recruit players for Major League teams. He was proud of my accomplishments throughout my career. My career with the American Legion became interesting when my best friend became my catcher. I became an explosive pitcher for the first couple of games. My coach approached me and heard that pro scouts were interested in my talents. My best friend Vance and I practice day and night to get ready for the pro scouts. We had a game the following Saturday against a great team from the west coast. My coach approached me and stated I would have to perform well that night, because the scouts were at the game looking at my every move.

The game started, and it was a close game until the eighth inning with the score 3-2 and us trailing. It was my turn to come up to bat. I waited for a good pitch and got one on the outside of the plate. I took the pitch to the right corner and hit the white line—a fair ball. I went around first base and approached second easily, but I decided to take third with a chance. I made it safe with a hard slide. I hurt my arm badly on the slide and had to go to the emergency room to get checked out. I broke my collar bone with the incident. I heard at the emergency room that we won the game due to my hit. I used the rest of the summer to get my strength back in my shoulder. I did therapy every day to get better. My career was over with the scouts; the time had come for me move up and get in the big leagues of high school. I had the whole summer to get ready to attend high school.

My mom couldn't provide for a lot of my school supplies, and I had to work in the tobacco fields for two months in order to pay for all of my school clothes. It was tough getting up five in the morning and working until 2:30 PM. I had to get home and immediately get dressed for football practices. I was the starting quarterback in tenth grade, but working in tobacco made often me late for practices. I had to walk or run about five miles every day to get there on time. I played a couple of games and performed very well. When I started coming late a lot, I lost my starting position. I was disappointed because I wanted to become a starting quarterback for a major college. I went to plan B: to become one of the best athletes at my high school. I had to work out hard in the weight room every day until my body hurt. The extreme pressure of getting a starting position with the team hit me.

My best friend would let me go to his house to get a lot of things off my mind. We go to his house and play spades.Cary and I would team up against his brother and dad. Sometimes we would even play his dad and his mom all day long. They always treated me as if I was part of the family. Cary and I thought we were so cool, and we would smoke weed, drink alcohol, and go to house parties. We used to walk to Boone's house and see what he was doing. We would meet his whole family: Paul, Martha (who was in my 1989 class), and his parents. His parents were true to the Lord like my mom. They were kin to some of the family members with whom I grew up inprojects. Everybody knew each other because we played sports together. I remember I had to use the bathroom and his dad came in the bathroom after me and stated, "Who in the world used the bathroom in here? They need to get cleaned out with some chemicals." Everyone started laughing. We always had fun, especially when he would fire up the grill outside. His dad would ask us, "You guys are crazy to be walking around with a big boom box on your shoulders, playing music real loud." That was the thing back then, especially with some cool sunglasses and a nice outfit with matching shoes.

When I returned to football practices, the coach decided to let his son become the starting quarterback. I began focusing on becoming a linebacker for the school. Overall, the season was great, and then it was time to get ready for basketball season. I was the superstar in basketball, scoring thirty points a game. I remember we took a trip to play out of town for the championship, and this girl watched me the whole time. When the game was over, she approached me and gave me her number. She said, "You played a great game, and my girlfriends and I were talking about you the whole game." On the way back to school on the bus, I started having fun. I got in the back of the bus, and one of the cheerleaders sat in the back with me. We started kissing, and I had some finger sex with her during the whole ride back. We return to the school safely.

Now it was time for baseball again. I continued to be a pitcher and a catcher for my high school. I became so good in baseball that everyone would come to the game to see me pitch. I was sixteen years old and throwing a ninety-four-miles-per-hour fastball. There weren't too many kids pitching at that speed in the late eighties. I continued to improve though the summer. When we weren't playing in games, we would go over Danny's house and take batting practice. All of teammates would stick together until we got better. Keith was my best friend throughout the baseball season, and we would go to his house to eat and hang out. Keith's mom treated me like a son. I want to thank the Jones family for their support.

The summer was great, and then I met this girl named Tonie. We started dating at the ball park. She used to come see her brother, Mike Williams, play every game. Then one day she saw me perform and fell in love with my style of play. We dated for a while at a young age. We broke up, and I started dating Allysa. I would go to Allysa's house before every game, and I would see my buddy's over there with the Johnson sisters. Allysa's cousin, Donna , would give me some advice to stay focused on my baseball career. Allysa and my cousins would come to my baseball game to see me play every game.

It was a good summer because my friends and I would go to the pool at Guy Smith Stadium. This was the place for everybody to go swimming and have a good time. The summer was good because I met back up with Allysa and she showed me where she lived. They moved closer to Fifth Street, near the Raven, which had the best chicken wings.

After football practices I would walk to Shelia Hedrick's house and spend a couple of hours with her. Her mom, Jet, was so cool and would let us spend the weekend together going out to different places. She would also let us spend some quiet time together at the Camelot Hotel, to get away from all of the town's drama. We would get in the room, watch a good movie, and listen to old-school music all night long. We fell in love and were making plans for the future, to go to college and get married after graduation. It didn't work out that way because we broke up over a big-time dope dealer in the neighborhood.

The summer was over, and now it was time to get ready for the eleventh grade. When you hit the eleventh grade, most colleges start looking at the best athletes in east coast. It was time for me to get focused on my academics as well. When football started, the coach decided to put me on the second team linebackers and tight ends, because I had gotten bigger from lifting weights during the off season. This was a big challenge because the twelfth graders were a lot bigger and stronger than I was. It was a talented team, with speed as well as strength. I became so stressed about getting a starting spot that I started drinking alcohol and smoking weed after the games. I remember riding with older guys and a couple of friends, heading to other small towns and talking to every girl at the clubs. We would smoke and drink the whole night. We met a couple of girls, and one of them took me to her mom's house and didn't hesitate about having sex with me.

I would go to different parties after the game. We would get together and ride around while getting high in the GP. The spot for the after party was close to my neighborhood, and one could hear the music at my house. I remember my best friend was trying to fight my young friend in the tenth grade, but he was the fast person on the team. When Black approached him, he took off running; the only thing we saw was the bottoms of his sneakers. When a fight broke out, the team stuck together at every party. We would come to the party with about twenty football players.

When I decided to get everything back on track on the field, the coach let me start at tight end. I was also the man for every punt return. I was pretty fast at 6'1" and 240 pounds. It put me back on track to get focused on the important stuff in the classroom, and I wanted the team to be undefeated throughout the season. I had a wonderful role model who saw potential in me. The high school coach would be concerned about our well-being, both on the field and in the classroom. I performed well on the kickoff team. I caught one of the biggest passes as a tight end and ran for about forty yards to give my team a winning chance in a good game. That's how my name got started in football. We went 10-0 for the season and then headed to the playoffs, where we lost in the second round in a close game.

It was time to get ready for basketball season again. I didn't get much playing time for some reason and lost interest in basketball, so I started focusing on getting bigger in the weight room. My best friend Black would walk to the weight room with me, and we'd work out the first chance we had. Every time we got there, we would see Randy and Willie, and both of them benched four hundred pounds. The season went well, but the record wasn't that good in basketball.

It was time to get ready for another wonderful year in baseball. We played a lot of teams in baseball with no competition. There was one game that was really close, and we needed a winning hit in the bottom of the eighth inning. The pitcher for the other team was one of the famous pitchers who played pro baseball in the early eighties. He got the count on me to 2-2, and then he threw me a curveball on the other side corner. I got into it and sent it four hundred feet over the left field wall to give us the winning run for the game. After the game, the pro player came and gave me a handshake, saying, "Good game, son. You are a wonderful talent for the future." That compliment gave me more confidence for the next season.

One time we had to travel to a high school to play against an undefeated team. It was the talk of the week in the newspaper. They had a pitcher named James Brunswick, and he was a hard thrower like me. I pitched for my high school this game. The whole game he was throwing ninety-five miles per hour, and I threw ninety-six. The game went down to the seventh inning with a score of 0-0. I made a mistake and hung a curveball, and Derrick Cradle hit it into the right corner and got to third base because he was fast on his feet. They scored, and the final score was 1-0. James Brunswick came up to me and said, "You are the first person to ever pitch that well against me." James Brunswick went on to pitch for in the pros for a good organization. It was a fun year on the high school team.

I continued to play baseball in the summer, but I had to get ready for football season because I was going to the twelfth grade. This was the year I needed to prove to everyone what hard work could do for a talented person. I went out and bought me some top-of-the-line equipment. I wanted to look good and play well at the same time. My teammates had plans to stick together in every game. We had a good quarterback, and he led us to a successful season. We had the best defense in the whole nation. I saw something in my little buddy in the eleventh grade. I would stay on him about every play. He did start at the beginning of the season, but when I finished with him, he became one the starters in the middle of the season. He thanked me for the support of believing in his talent.

One game against a team from out of town, this guy tried to catch a pass, I hit him so hard the ambulance came and took him off of the field. That was the turning point in my career. Everybody from my neighborhood came to my games, and they would hear my name loud and clear from the announcer.

In the middle of the season we developed a problem with our star running back, who hurt his knee. He had played with the big boys ever since he was in the tenth grade. He was so good that the crowd would go crazy when he did flips in the end zone after a touchdown. However, now he was out for the rest of the season. During his injury the coach would ask me to play running back and linebacker, and special teams, too. I did it to support my team. I was getting tired by playing both positions all game long. My name became so popular that I started dating one of the finest girls in school. Her name was Allison, and she was short and sexy. I got brave one time and decided to meet her parents during the school year.

The coach sat everybody down and explained, "We will be facing the best team in the eastern area. The team is Dunbar, which is 9-0, and we are 9-0. The winner will be the champion for the season." The game started with a tight score. It seemed like the team was studying my every move at running back.

At half time I pulled everybody together and said, "We came a long way together, and we can't lose this game. I know everybody is tired, but we've got two more quarters. I will take everyone on my shoulders. I worked too hard all year to lose this game." We started the third quarter with a new attitude about the game. We played well and kept the game tight. It would to take a good play to win this game. It happened with two minutes left. Coach came to me and said, "Malik, we are giving you ball."

We got in the huddle, and I said to everyone, "It's time to celebrate. Meet me in the end zone." I got the ball and got a block from Danta and Monty, and I got in the clear so that I could see who was next to get past. I made a nice move on one guy, and there was one guy left before the end zone. One of my teammates came out of nowhere and hit him. I ran down the sideline fifty yards to win the game. When I crossed the end zone, the whole crowd called my name for fifteen minutes. It felt good because all of the hard work had just paid off for my team. The whole school gave me the nickname the Superstar. After the game a couple of guys and I went home, changed clothes, and got dressed for the after party at the Diamonds. There were a lot of people there, but we stayed outside to catch all the women and drink some beer. Everybody came up to me and congratulated me on the winning touchdown. I had a couple of woman trying to give me their numbers, but I was faithful to my girlfriend, Allison.

At the next practice, we got ready for the playoffs. The local news came out and asked me what we were going to do to Pine Forest. I stated, "We are going to cut their trees down." We lost in the playoffs, but my teammates thanked me for a wonderful season. They stated, "You never gave up on us." The season was over.

I started to focus on my education so that I could go to a good school. I played basketball but wasn't dedicated to playing the whole season. I got an offer at a good college to go for two years to get my grades back on track. I enjoyed the rest of senior year and took my girlfriend to the prom. We got a limo with Tommy and Laura, and the four of us had a good time riding in the limo and going out to eat. We arrived at the prom and danced all night.

It was time to get ready for graduation. I remember there was this motivational speaker who came to the school to speak to everyone about drunk driving and doing drugs. He was driving drunk one night, got in an accident, and lost both of his legs. I wish I had listened to him more; he was trying to tell me the importance of life.

I went to graduation and enjoyed the rehearsal in the morning. When it was time to walk across stage, it was a wonderful day because the announcer started calling the names, and the crowd yelled loudly. The crowd calmed down until they called my name. When they called my name, the auditorium stood up and yelled. They remembered all the good things I done for the school.

After the graduation I had a lot of parties to attend. I met Wendy at one of the parties, and she took me home on Chestnut.

My mom had moved to a different location before I graduated from high school. We pulled in my mom's driveway and talked all night before I got ready to take a trip to the beach. My English teacher rewarded our class with a field trip at the end of the year: we went to beach. I took my girlfriend, Allison. We started having problems when she saw me and some other guys talking to a group of girls, and we broke up on the trip. We had plans to go to the same college and graduate at the same time. I want to thank my classmates for a wonderful year in school and some great moments.

# III. Street Life

I made it through high school with a smile on my face. I finally played baseball at the semi-pro level. I then came back to my mom's house and started hanging out with a friend of mine who lived down the street. We drank beer and partied all the time. I lost focus on trying to attend a college while I had the chance. We would hang out at different clubs on a daily basis. During this time the best singing group was out at Diamonds, and they were the talk of the town. I went to school with these guys and played baseball with some of them, so I would get in free at every event.

I would see Tammy at all of the Diamonds' parties. She would always come up to me and ask me, "How are you doing tonight?" Some guys from the neighborhood were famous for selling drugs, and women would go crazy when they attended the party. They had the cars and the women. The thing that made me feel good was when they saw me, we would talk about all the games on the field. They used to love seeing me play, especially when they had a lot of money on the game. I remember Sweet Dee, the biggest dealer, bought me some brand-new shoes for one of the games; they would bring up things like that. The club scene got so bad that I would pick fights because I was tough and a lot people were scared of me. When I didn't hang with Rod, I would go to Sammy's house or be at my family's house to see if they were cooking out that day. My family always had a good time every weekend.

When I would leave my cousin's house, Sammy would want to drink a couple of beers, and he would call Maurice and Big Tee to drink with us. These were the two biggest guys in Greenville at the time, except for Baby Hulk. We had a good time talking about the times when they would come to my games. We had a couple more guys who would come through and drink with us, and they were Al and Joe. We would drink until everyone passed out. I would leave when Cherry would come by and pick me up, and we would ride and talk about different life experiences and what we planned on doing in the future. Cherry and I became really close, so one day I decided to go my favorite barbershop and get her name cut in the back of my hair. I had some strong feelings for her at the time because she would always encourage me to make something out of myself. She made a brother feel good about life.

One day J-Rod came up on a bicycle and asked me to ride with him to the liquor store to get some good stuff. He convinced me to buy some old whisky from the 1800s. I bought everything else and started riding the bike back to the spot to get started on the whisky. It went straight to the head, but it didn't hit me until I drove my friend's car to the store to get some more beer. When I got back to the spot, I parked the car, stepped out, and fell back in a fence about forty feet away from a house. I was so drunk that Maurice had to take me home and drop me off. My mom was mad about the situation, but she didn't say anything until she got back from church.

The next morning when I woke up, my stepdad started tripping about the night before. My mom took his side and told me to get out. I packed all my things and stayed with my friend Dewanda; she welcomed me in with open arms. I stayed there for a couple of weeks until I called a friend, Elie Teel, about getting a place of our own. He agreed, so we moved to a reasonable place until we could do better. We got a job at the same place, a grocery store. We got along very well with bills and food.

We were working one day, and this guy named Darryl was complaining about his girlfriend, who was trying to put him out on the street. We decided to let him move in and get his stuff together. We had problems with him at first because he didn't want to work. We had a good time, though, because I was dating a girl from the local university named Tasha. Darryl was trying to date her roommate, but she didn't like light-skinned guys. We still had fun with the university students. We would have cookouts and attend all of the pool parties in the complex. My cousin Stacy and his crew would come through the area with their Jeeps in a row. We would travel out of town to an awesome homecoming and to the beach every year.

We made a big mistake when we let a guy name Tee-Love move in. He started causing different conflicts with different neighbors. We still had a good time going to different university parties and to Cotton Hall, where all the football players had fun. We stayed there for a couple more years, and then we had to move out. I went back to my mom's house, and Elie Teel went to his grandparents' house. I don't know where the other guys went. When I returned home, my friends showed me some love, and we decided to go out that night to celebrate. We went to the hottest club, which was right around the corner from Shelia Hendricks' house. I went by to speak and noticed her mom was sitting on the porch. She said Shelia Hendricks had been asking about me. Her boyfriend was not working out because of his lifestyle in the drug game. I found they were moving close to my area. When they moved, she came over to see me. At the time I was seeing Cherry. We didn't work out, so I went over to Shelia Hendricks' house, and we had a serious talk. We agreed to do better.

I started hustling and delivered dope to the block without anybody knowing. I made a mistake and sold to an undercover cop, and I tried to make it through the field back to Shelia Hendricks' house. The police surrounded me and took me to jail. I got my first record. I went to court and got probation, with eight months in prison if I made a mistake. I didn't take it seriously and wouldn't go to meetings. I started smoking weed on a daily basis. My probation officer caught me and sent me to prison for the first time in my life. When Shelia Hendricks heard I was going to prison, she didn't want to be a part of it; she broke up with me before I left for prison. When I arrived at prison, I didn't know what to expect. I knew a lot of guys from my hometown, but I hadn't seen them in a long time. It was an unusual experience. I couldn't use the bathroom when I wanted to, and most guys would try to fight you over little things, like a hair comb. I saw a guy get stabbed over some food at 6:30 in the morning. In the back of my mind I thought, *It's too early for this.*

I hung around one of the old school guys, and he gave me some advice for when I would get out of prison. He had got twenty years for a crazy shooting in my hometown. The advice he gave

26

was, "Never let your pride keep you hungry." I also got advice from this old man named Mr. Patterson. He was serving fifty years as big-time dope dealer in the early eighties. I stayed focused and lifted weights because that was my passion, and time passed more quickly.

It was soon time for me to go home. I got picked up and went straight to a hotel to have a good time. I haven't had sex in eight months. When I arrived home, everybody had a party for me. While I was at the cookout, I was asking question about the corner. I found that one of the boys from out of state, named Quincy, had started selling drugs around the corner. The thing about the streets is that people will get jealous and try to get you knocked for making money on their territory. I decided to start my own thing around the corner from these guys. I didn't know too much about the streets, so I went to an old friend to get the scoop about hustling and the street life. I started out small because I didn't know anybody in the game. The guys I knew from the projects, the ones who used to come to my games, were dead or locked up for a long time. It was a slow process because everybody was on the other side of town. I made a special trip to where I grew up, and I advertised my special for everybody. I think everybody wanted to find out whether it was true that they could buy two and get one free. I built my business up with 150 dollars. The drug game was just like selling products wholesale: it was supply and demand to the consumer. I started reading books on all the mistakes old gangsters had made in the past. It took me two months to double my money. In the game it was all about how quickly you flipped the first couple of packages, unless you were selling major weight. I was grinding from the bottom to the top. I guess the word got out about the two for one deal on the block, because it was getting better. Most of the old street hustlers were getting caught on a daily basis. In a two-month period, it was time to see the man with three hundred dollars of merchandise. I was moving up the ladder slowly.

In the process of making this money, I met this girl named Delicious. She had been in the game for a while. We became close because she needed someone to babysit her daughter while she was running the streets. My mom kept her daughter for ten years until Delicious got herself together. My mom loves kids and is an amazing women with a pure soul. I told Delicious I needed a ride or die chick on my team, someone who already knew the game and knew more people to deal with in the future. It worked out well because with her information, I got to six hundred dollars in three months. It is a lot of grinding when you're starting from the bottom. The main thing is having the right connections to keep you supplied throughout your journey.

Life was getting better. I moved in with Delicious, and we started pulling together. We came up with an idea to get a beeper for better communication, so I wouldn't have to stay on the corner as much. She said, "Keep grinding hard until you get to a thousand dollars." The beeper was for the important people when it came to business. We didn't have cell phones, so when someone called me on the beeper, I had to use a payphone booth. I finally got to a thousand dollars and got a better connection. He gave a deal: anytime I bought one, I got another up front. So out of four thousand dollars of product, I only had to give him a thousand dollars to start with. Street life was getting better.

At this time my mom moved around the corner, closer to my block. It was a nice, laid-back place to have some cookouts. I had come up with an idea to get this product out faster, so I had to find to people to trust and who were willing to be serious in the game. I talked to my cousin Zee and a guy known as the Grinder, and they agreed to make money on the strip. It was getting so that good people came from places out of town because I had a good connection. We went shopping every day and stayed in different hotels, especially the hotels with breakfast buffets, which were the spots for all of the big ballers.

This girl I knew from a while back was at one hotel, and we had sex. When I finished I decided to go get something to eat. I saw two friends I hadn't seen for a while, Top Dog and Big Money. These were some cool guys. I had to go the best spot in town to get my sub close to the baseball field. I would pay for a hotel for me and the boys for a week. The money brought different women to the hotels. It started moving so fast that I had to get some guns for protection. I purchased five pistols and put them in a safe. I wanted to expand my business, so I got two more people on my corner. I wanted to move out of town with this product because it was the best in town at the time. The other crew member was some straight hustler who just needed an opportunity. That was what the streets loved about me: when I ate, everybody got a piece of the pie.

I decided to walk to the home a friend named Adrian, who was a true hustler. When we were walking home, we talked about expanding dope to the city and being bigger than Nino. I agreed and walked him all the way home. I told him, "You are feeling good because we smoked a blunt on the way. Go in the house and don't come out until tomorrow." He agreed, and I went home to Delicious, went to sleep, and woke up to some good breakfast.

I received a phone call from my cousin, who told me to turn on the news. They found Adrain dead in the hotel last night; he had overdosed on drugs. I said, "I told him to stay in the house." I decided to take Delicious on a nice vacation to let her know I appreciated her understanding and commitment to my organization, and to get away for a while.

The street life on my block became very intense, especially the nightlife. The nightlife was unlike anything I had seen before. There were so many cars coming though: dope heads, gold diggers, police, and robbers. I had three women working for me as a detour for high-profile workers and lawyers—whoever had the big money. I would send my girls over to their houses with the drugs, to comfort them with product and women. I decided to get some walkie talkies and put guys on each corner.

I had one experience where some guys came from out of town wanting to buy some weight. I always carried one pistol. The out of town boss gets out of the car and meets me on the side of the house—I never did business in the house. I had a huge block so that I could see everything. These boys tried to rob me not, realizing it was my turf. I had to shoot one of them in the stomach and the other one in the knee. I didn't want to kill them on my block. My crew beat them back into the car, and I was surprised they made it out of the hood. After that situation I got two troopers to carry pistols everywhere we went. I didn't want to tell my cousin Marlo about the incident because he would've shut down the whole block. It was a challenge every day on the block.

One guy name Nutty smoked dope all day. He didn't have money, so he came to me and asked me if I needed anything done that day, so that he could get high. I said, "Come on, let's go to my mom's house and see if she needs anything." He found out she needed a refrigerator and decided to get her a new one. I made a deal with him. "If you get the refrigerator, I'll give you enough work to last you for three days." He left, running south of the block. I didn't pay it any mind and bought a case of Budweiser for the block.

We were drinking when someone said, "What is Nutty doing with a dolly and a refrigerator, coming down the block?" I said that it was for my mom. I asked him to go set it up because my mom was not home. I gave him enough to last a while, and he took off running again.

I met this young lady from upstate named Wanda. She was very pretty and down to earth. She decided to stay with me one night, and we were being romantic upstairs in my room when my cousin threw a rock at the window, talking about how he needed more work and one of the guns. I gave him enough to last two days. This night we were the only ones in this half of the town with dope. We sold almost fifteen thousand dollars worth of dope in three days. Wanda and I had to go to a hotel so that no one could find us, because she was going back upstate in a couple of days. We enjoyed the next couple of days by relaxing and being romantic. The whole block was looking for me every day. She finally went back to her hometown; I stayed in contact with her through Flute and her family. Her brother always came to the block to see how I was doing.

My cousin Kevin, a.k.a. Dopeman, started coming from across town to hang with me. We became really close over the next couple of months. The crew kept the block going, but Dopeman, Zee, and I would go to the mall and get hotel rooms to get away. We would meet women at the mall and take them out to the clubs before heading back to the hotel to have sex. We went to the club one night at the Platinum, and we met some girls from out of town.

They want to have some fun after the club. We took them to one of the nicest breakfast spots in my town, and I kept my eye on this girl named Shoranda the whole night. She wasn't into the fame and money; she was more laid back and wanted to have a good time. We exchanged number and talked on the phone all the time. She would come down with her cousins, especially Monica, and they were like two sisters. I became close to these two girls. I remember they took a cab fifty miles to my town just to see me. That meant a lot to me. Shoranda and I became closer every day. We decided to get a room one day and talk about the future. I stated I wanted to have sex with her. She told me she was a virgin. It made me pause for a minute, because she was pure, but we still had sex. We connected and entered a relationship, talking every day on the phone.

The money was coming so fast that I knew something was wrong with the streets. I found out that the boys had run out of drugs on Harris Avenue and needed some over there. Harris Avenue was the million-dollar spot back in the days. It was a dream for me to be invited over there. I left everybody over on the block except my cousin Dopeman. Dopeman and I went over to Harris Avenue and posted in a good area. The money was coming so quickly that I didn't know what to do.

A tow truck pulled up and wanted something. It was a crackhead named Nicole, and everybody from my neighborhood knew her. She spent 250 dollars when she saw us. My cousin said, "I want to go see where the rest of the money with them is. I'm leaving with them for a few minutes." Nicole had some more women at the house.

I said, "Just leave me the gun so I can protect myself." The truck drove off to the north.

Thirty minutes later this boy named Takeoff rolled up on me, shook my hand, and said he wanted to make some money tonight. I replied, "If you make me some money, I will give you something every time after the sale." He made about a thousand dollars, and I gave him 150. The night went on, and the moon was getting kind of dark—it didn't feel right. The money slowed down. The crackheads started coming up to me with short money every time. I kept a lookout because I knew the situation. A white car pulled up,

31

and a boy and came to me and said they wanted to spend a hundred dollars. I showed him three hundred dollars worth of dope, and he hit my hand, knocked the dope in the air, and caught it before he started running. I waited until he got in the clear and shot him three times. The street code is not to let anyone take anything from you. I packed everything up and walked back toward my block.

On my way I saw my cousin Marlo at a sports bar. He asked, "What is wrong with you?"

I explained, "I just shot a boy three times."

He said, "So what? Let's go get a drink. Did he try to take something from you?" I stated yes. He replied, "Let's go get fucked up, then." We drank and laughed until dawn.

I jumped in a cab and went to Delicious' house. She told me, "Takeoff got shoot on Harris Avenue." I couldn't lie, so I told her the truth. We stayed glued to the news and had friends at the hospital to get the results. He didn't die—what a relief. The next morning I went back to the block to explain to the boys I might have to go away and do some time; everything would be run though Delicious and Dopeman until I got back. I did thirty months for the crime. I stayed in contact with Shorando, and she wrote me and told me the block was still going when I wasn't there. I did my time and got out to see about the block. I got the boys together to see how Shorando was doing. We decided to take a trip to visit her in her small town, about fifty miles away. When I arrived in her town, I found out she had a boyfriend. I had lost her. I had been too focused on the game and had lost a good girl by chasing money. I didn't see Shorando after that. I went back to my hometown hurt, but I didn't let the boys see my weakness because I was a boss. Dopeman felt my pain.

I returned to the block like it was yesterday. I had a huge coming home cookout party. The block was not the same because one day I saw ten Mustangs of different colors drive though the block. I thought, *The big boys are in town to close the block down.* It was time to get another spot. I was standing on the block enjoying the weather when Delicious said, "I have some people in a different state that want to meet you." She always looked after my best interests. She taught me the game every day. She was my good bad girl—very educated and street smart. The boys came down and liked the setup I had on my block. They wanted to invest in a new spot. I invited them to my spot, where we could get the best fish sandwiches in town. I stated, "I will be better off coming to your hometown as a new face, because I'm a natural hustler. I can go anywhere and make a dollar out of fifteen cents." They agreed to come get me in three weeks. That gave me enough time to explain everything to my crew; I stated that when I got settled, I'd come back and show some love to them. My crew was hurt, but they had a going away party for me that lasted two days. I didn't sleep for three days—we were up for two days doing a lot of cocaine.

I remember the boys pulled up in the yard, and I grabbed my luggage to put in the truck. I couldn't believe I was making a new start for my life. We arrived in their hometown, in the middle of the hood. I was full of nerves because I didn't know these guys that well. We arrived late, so we dropped the bags off and went straight to bed. The next morning they showed love: a beautiful girl brought me breakfast in the bed, and after I ate, she had sex with me. I couldn't believe it—these boys were big time. I took a shower, got dressed, and went out back where everyone was in the pool. The boys pulled me aside and said, "We are going to let you meet everybody until you get the feel of the game here."

I wasn't there a month until I got my own personal people and had five different girlfriends in town. The thing that got me was that they knew about each other, but they didn't care as long I was paying their bills. They would let me keep my stashes at their houses. I fell in love with this one girl who worked at a law firm. That was the boss lawyer for me and the crew, if something went wrong. She would be professional at the office until she got home. She would bring different tools out of the closet that were freaky. I could see it in her eyes when I first met her that she wanted me. When I walked up, she said, "You are a sexy black man." That was all I needed to hear. She was sexy as hell and always smelled good. I think I had a son with her, but I never got the information from her. Everyone kept telling me about it, and a young boy came to my hometown looking for me with a similar face.

33

The game was different in these boys' hometown—it was like candy once one got to know it. I would stand out in front of a popular eating spot on the east side and would make five thousand dollars in one night. This is a true story. I had my own personal people, and they had big houses and snorted cocaine. I remember one day this guy called me and said, "I've got some money but I'll give you my wife for the rest of the product." I couldn't believe it. I mean, she had a body like a sister and was beautiful. I couldn't resist this offer. I took his wife in the room and had sex with for about two hours. I left and gave him extra for this service.

I left and then got a call on the north side of town for four and a half ounces. I went to a stash, grabbed a paper bag, and went out the door. I arrived at this girl's house with whom I was having sex on a regular basis. The guys would be there to get the coke. I noticed something was wrong when an extra guy came this time. It didn't seem right, so I put my gun in my waistband. I walked in the house, and one guy came from behind the door and tried to choke me. I shot him until he went down and continued to shoot the whole crew without asking question. I started to shoot the chick, but her sex was the boom. I didn't go on that side of the town for a while. I called the girl and told her to meet me at the hotel. I asked her whether she'd heard anything about that went down. She stated, "I was trying to make some money, too."

I brought this incident to my boss. He was mad and said, "I'm going to deal with these guys personally." I didn't hear anything about this situation anymore.

I got a call from some girls who wanted to hang out at my place and make sure I was okay after the incident. They would cook, make sure my crib stayed straight, and feed my fish every day. I would stop by on a regular basis to see if my boss was okay about everything.

One day I stopped by there, and his crazy son Terry was in the house playing video games. He was a cool guy, but he really loved the street activities a lot more than me and his dad. He was known for shooting people for no reason at all. He didn't believe in anything but the streets. He asked me to hang out with him, so I decided to take the chance of going deeper in the streets. It was an awesome day because he turned me on to some more dope people in the game, and we decided to go to the club later that night. I had a great time because I hadn't been out in a couple of years. The last time I had been out was when I had that conflict in my hometown, when the guy at the club tried to kill me. After the club we went back to my crib, where we drank some gin and juice and smoked on some good marijuana with three beautiful women. It turned into an all-nighter; after getting high, we got hungry and went to a spot in his town called Big Mama's Burgers. We took the food back to my crib and every enjoyed the rest of the night.

The next morning my drug connection called me and said he needed to talk to me about something important right away. I went to Terry's daddy's place, where he joined me for some breakfast. Me and his daddy went to the backyard, and he asked me whether I would be interested in boxing, because he saw what I did to one guy when he didn't pay me my money. I said, "Sure, but who is going to sponsor me?"

He replied, "I am, and I have you a trainer. His name is Houston, and he used to be a heavyweight champion back in the days."

I was excited about the situation and started eating different types of foods. It didn't stop my hustling; flow money still came in. On my first day of training, I had to get up at 5:00 AM and start running up the hills in this town while drinking egg yolk throughout the process. The running came first—I didn't see any ring training until a month later. When I started ring training, Houston was very serious about every move and the way I positioned my body. He had me boxing with a unique style. He would teach me how to cut off fighters in the ring. I learned a lot compared to fighting in the streets.

I learned in the street how to knock out people with one punch and not used technique and power. My buddy Hitman in Greenville showed me how to fight on command. I trained for about six months until I had my first fight, and I won in the third round with a knockout. My boss took me out to celebrate with all of the old dealers. They were so proud of me winning them some money that night, and they gave me a nickname, One Hitter Quitter. I was become well-known throughout the city. I was still getting my hustle on, but I had to let the girls run the dope for me. These ladies were loyal to the game. I would buy them anything they wanted from any store. I continued to train hard every day until my next fight. I won three more fights in a three-month period. I fought for one year, and then Houston wouldn't show up because I found out he was using drugs. I went to John's house one day to see what was going on, and Houston stated getting high was more important to him right now.

I decided to get deep into the game after this took place. I started with distribution drugs to clients in different cities. Life was getting better. I started counting stacks of money on a daily basis. It got so good that I got a second crib with a huge aquarium and blue fish. I decided to take trips to some beautiful places that I couldn't have imagined a few years earlier. It was the first time I got on an airplane. I got a small plane to the next city over and another to my destination. This showed me there was more to life than staying in a small town and getting locked up. I arrived at the airport in forty-five minutes. When I decided to walk through the tunnel to get to my flight, I noticed an old friend from my high school. We talked for a minute and exchanged information. When I got to my part of the airport, I saw a famous track star who was the fastest woman in the world at that time. I received an autograph from her.

They called my flight, and I nervously got on the plane. My friends told me to relax and enjoy the moment. We arrived at my destination within two hours. It was a great flight with Coke and peanuts. When I went through the tunnel, I saw a professional basketball player standing about seven feet tall. He was the talk of the city. I ran over to him and got another autograph from a superstar.

My boss's people had a limo waiting for us out front to see some of his people. We rode with a crazy guy who took us over by the old football stadium. It was hot as hell in this town—it was even hot in the air conditioning. We got settled in the hotel room before dinner. The next day we went to the mall to find something to wear out to the club that night. The mall was packed with a lot of Spanish women. I didn't see any other race. We rode around to sight see and explore the palm trees on the beach. We then met up with my boss's people, and he had a surprise for us. We had two women apiece in a separate room. I had a good time with these beautiful women. We took care of business and arrived back at my hustling spot.

When I landed at the airport, everyone told me Delicious had arrived in town. I got in my truck and drove to the neighborhood to see how she was doing. When I saw her, I noticed she was a little upset about the situation and said we needed to talk. She said, "I thought you were coming here to just make money, not to fuck everything in the city."

I replied, "Are you serious? It's not a good time. We are getting ready to make some major money."

I put her in one of the expensive hotel in town for a month. I didn't know if she was going to stay or leave. When I was driving, I started thinking about who could've told her about the other women. I was telling a friend that stayed a couple of blocks from me all of my business, so she must had called back home and told everyone, and then it got back to Delicious. I didn't let it bother to me and I got back on my grind. I noticed I didn't get a call from Delicious for a couple of hours, and I decided to go check on her. I arrived at the hotel and opened the door with my key, and I noticed it was quiet in the room. She was in the bathroom in the tub, trying to kill herself underwater. I got their just in time. When she got herself together, I asked her why she did that. She stated, "I love you, and I don't want anyone to have you." I didn't know she liked me that much; I thought we were just business partners. We talked about it and decided to rent a truck and take her back to our hometown. I made a couple of calls and asked my cousin to get everybody together so that we could have a good time. I brought about nine ounces with me to my hometown. I gave some work away and sold most of it to twin boys. I stayed there for a week and then went back to my money spot out of town.

When I arrived back, I called my boss, and he said he needed to talk to me about something. He stated he was getting hot by the police, so he need a lieutenant to handle some tasks. He wanted me to learn about all of his pit bulls, because he kept his product under the doghouse. I started walking them and feeding them every day until they got used to me. I could get any amount of drugs and take whatever I wanted as long the money was correct.

The police got really hot on his tail, so he shut the block down. I didn't have a connection anywhere, so I packed up and explained to everyone, "My time is up in this town." I thanked them for the opportunity to learn. There was more in the world to offer, good or bad; one had to take a chance on success. I packed everything up and moved back to my hometown.

When I arrived, everyone was ready to party. I went to one of my old hotel spots and bought five rooms on the same floor. I saw my cousin Spotty G having a party on the floor. I went to his room and looked out the window. I saw this girl looking like a beautiful celebrity. I went down the stairs, cut her off, and put the mack down on her. I got her number and name: Lexus. I asked her, "What are you doing up here?"

She replied, "I'm visiting my boyfriend."

I partied with the fellows for three days straight. I went to my mom's house to relax and visit family and friends. As I was relaxing, Delicious came over to show me some love. We hung out all night and had a good time After getting a room away from everybody. We had sex like it was the last day we'd see each other. We had a long conversation about not seeing each other for a while. I called her a cab to get home. I was developing feelings for Lexus. When I returned to my mom's house and gave Lexus a call, I asked whether she could meet me at my mom's house sometime that day. I decided to move in with my mom until I had plans to make my next move to get money. I had my own room, so I had my privacy to do whatever I wanted to do. My friends didn't hear from me for a while because I was trying to do something different in my life. They didn't come around when Lexus came around, because she didn't yet know my lifestyle.

Delicious came by one day unexpectedly and met Lexus. Delicious threw her hands up and said she didn't want anything else to do with me. After that incident Lexus and I became really close. Her car was in the shop, so she would get the milk man to drop her off at my house to stay a couple of days. It became a huge issue because her mom thought she was at her friend's house from school. She was very strict with Lexus's well-being. It was very understandable because I would be concerned about my daughter around a thug. When she went home, we would talk on the phone all night, planning our future. She had me so focused about life that I was thinking about going back to college, but I was so used to the fast money; it was in my blood at the time. I didn't want her to know that I was a hustler in the streets.

I also didn't want to hustle on that side of town because people were getting killed on the regular basics. I didn't know a lot of people on that side of town, but they knew me from my old block. I was walking to the store one day, and an old friend, Laquita, asked me to ride around with her. We rode through my old block to see who was out, and I was thankful for the ride because I needed to get out of the house. I saw a lot of my family members in the area. My old block became the million-dollar spot when I was over there. I didn't start a block on that side of town because I was more like a flow hustler on the streets. It was a billion dollars because they sold everything on these spots. I would walk to the store and see heroin addicts leaning over high crackheads, breaking into people's houses in the daylight. Killers were ready to rob anyone with big packs. It was just like living in my old block, with gunshots popping in the air all the time. I was trying to get involved in this life again, so I worked off of my pager. When my pager went off I would walk to the store with a payphone next to the Platinum Club.

When I wasn't hustling, Lexus would come over, and we would walk downtown to the boardwalk holding hands and enjoying each other. She was more like a country girl and was not used to the city life. She was a sweet young girl who was ready for an adventurous experiences. We dated for a couple of months, and then I told her that I was a hustler from the streets. I thought she was going to leave, but she wanted to experience some of the street life. I asked her, "Are you ready for this crazy life?" She said yes. She finally got her car out of the shop, so when someone would call me for some weight, she would take me to their house. When we arrived, I asked her, "Would you like to come in to see how these people sit around a table smoking dope?" I saw one guy playing a guitar and thinking he was an old country singer from back in the days. A black guy was looking out the window like his wife was going to show up and catch him smoking crack; he kept telling everybody to be quiet. The thing about crackheads in a house is that there is one big-time crackhead that controls the whole house. He feels like he has a million dollars in his pocket.

Lexus came in to see all of the crackheads blowing out the smoke, and when she inhaled some of that smoke, she ran back to the car. I took care of my business, and when I went outside I asked her, "Are you okay?"

She said, "I will not be going in there anymore."

We would go shopping and keep her car running well. She started seeing me count a couple of thousand dollars in her face. We use to take rides out of town to get away from the street life. The longer she stayed away from her mom, the situation between them was more complicated, and she couldn't get money. I would call her to come over, and for some reason her keys would go missing, so she couldn't drive. Instead, we would stay on the phone all night talking.

When Lexus didn't come to town, I would go visit my old friends in the projects, where I grew up as a youth. These guys were older than me and would give me some good insight about life. While I was in the area, I ran into the hustler of the year, Hustleman. I used to watch him play basketball; he reminded me of a professional basketball player that is playing right now. He stated I was doing well in the dope with that weight, and he asked, "Do you think we can hook up sometime? I know a lot of people that smoke dope." Hustleman was a true old-school hustler who worked all day and night to get that money. He would teach me how to stick and move in the dope game. "Never stay in the same place too long, and never drive back the same way on a major delivery," he'd say. I wondered whether he ever slept.

We did pretty well the first week hustling together on the street. He knew people with real money. It was good times in the hood, and we cooked out and showed love together with no shooting over a dollar. My business expanded very well, so I would put Hustleman in the cross-town area. He would flow all night with me and give me all of my money; he was a loyal gangster to me.

One day he said, "We can't keep driving the same car around town, making money. The police will pick up on our whereabouts."

I said, "Let me a rent a car and drive around."

He said, "Cool, but I have the perfect place."

I thought he was talking about a rental company. He was talking about renting someone's personal car. That was how wild he was in the hood. We visited this guy's house whom he'd known for a long time and who had done drugs for a long time. Hustleman would always go in the house and get the guys started by letting them get a hit of his dope. This would trigger the brain, and the crackhead would do anything for another hit. Hustleman was smooth when it came to getting something done. The guy let us rent the car for a week; we would stop by and give him some more dope on a regular basis. We sold so much dope out of that car that the vehicle started having problems.

Hustleman and I became so close, and he stated that one day he was going get his life on track and get back with his wife. I believed him, but he was in the game too deep. He would run the street for three weeks without any sleep. I had to get my eight hours a day, or I would not sell one piece of dope. One reason I'm writing this book is to thank my friends Hustleman and Dopeman, who were loyal to me every step of the way.

The only problem was that crackheads had him doing things he didn't want to do. I had seen that crackheads take the best of them down. I used to buy rooms so we could get away from everybody and get some rest. We would go shopping with my cousin Kevin, aka Dopeman. I would call Lexus to let her know I had a room, and I asked if she would come spend some quality time with me. She was happy to get away for a couple of hours. She would show up just when I was getting out of the shower and getting dressed. When she arrived, I went shopping for her and me for some new summer clothes. We then laid in the room relaxing, watching movies, and romancing all night.

I decided to go check on Hustleman because I hadn't heard anything from him for a couple of days. I went in his room, and he was sleeping like a baby from all of the running. I decided it was time for Hustleman and Lexus to meet. It was a little scary, but it worked out well. They became close because when she couldn't find me, she would go to Hustleman or Dopeman to find me.

I really enjoyed the three days off within the grind. Every hustler has to take time off to enjoy life. However, it was time to hit the streets again, and so Lexus went home with all of her presents and called me every day to see what was going on in the street. The streets always had a different story to tell—someone getting busted or shot. I decided to go to my mom's house to visit my stepdaughter, take them shopping, and spend more time with everyone. Hustleman went to his dad and mom's house to go fishing with his dad. We agreed to get back to together the next day, to take the car back to the owner. The guy was so excited to see us and his car in a good condition. We decided to change cars and get a renter car to visit everybody, to let them know we were back on the grind.

I was getting low on dope, and Nut decided to call one of his connections. He was worried because he knew I had that cash on hand to get whatever I wanted. He called an old friend who had been in the game for a while and had the best product in town. We met up and conducted business in a proper matter without any distraction. I bought enough to last for a couple of months. I bought cocaine because Hustleman was the best cook in town when it came to putting that crack together. We decided to cook the product at a friend's house. It was taking so long that I decided to call my cousin Dopeman over to drink a couple of beers with me and smoke some weed until everything was done. We had a good time reminiscing, but the thing about marijuana was that it made me lose focus on the most important things. I liked smoking it when I relaxed with a female friend because it increase my sex drive tremendously. When everything was cooked and bagged, I decided to give enough for the night and put the rest in the stash and continue to party with my cousin. Dopeman and I decided to hit the mall and get new outfits for the club that night. We went to the Blazing Club, which was fifty miles from our hometown. I saw a lot of my old friends and decided to buy a round of drinks at the bar. We had a good time partying all night, and then we decided to go to the after-party hangout at this restaurant that served good country food every day.

Dopeman and I decided to get a room at the across the street, because we had met to females at the club, and they wanted to spend the night. We got to the room, ate, smoked some more marijuana, and downed some mixed drinks. All of this led to us having sex for two days with these girls. They didn't want to go home, and so we took them shopping. I woke up the next morning after dropping my cousins off, and those girls I decided to go to my mom's house, where she was cooking some old-school cheese biscuits and a home-style breakfast. When you are in the streets real deep, you don't often have time to eat a home-cooked meal.

I called my whole crew to get ready, because I would be giving everybody a huge package of drugs today. I went by to check on Hustleman, and he was finished with the last package, so I had to get some bags to get everybody ready for the weekend and the first and fifteenth of the month.

While I was in the store, I ran across one of my old friends, B-Nice, and he wasn't looking to good. He said that he couldn't find a job, so he wanted to get a package of drugs from me. We used to hang out when I was younger, and we sold dope together on my old block. I explained to him how most guys have gone up on the prices for ounces in the whole town. He said, "I have a cousin in and out of town, and he could get the drugs a lot cheaper, if you would buy a large quantity." I asked him to let me know in a couple of days if he could get the deal together. I received a call from B-Nice at the beginning of the next week, and it was official. I finished everything, got all my money together, and was ready for a trip out of town. I was so excited to finally get some dope for cheaper prices—that meant I could double my money when I got back. The street code is never let anyone know your next move, because there are snitches everywhere. I called Lexus and asked her whether she wanted to take the trip out of town with me for a couple of days, to go shopping and sightseeing. I got with Hustleman and let him know I had an emergency that came up. "I'm leaving everything with you until I get back." I always put trust in Hustleman and Dopeman to take care of business. I got a room before I left so that we could make sure everything was in order before we left; I didn't making mistakes in the hustling game.

We all stayed in the same room together, and B-Nice called a friend over so he wouldn't be lonely while Lexus and I made love. We all got up at the same time in the morning and ate some wonderful breakfast from a place that sold good cheese and eggs. We pulled up to the gas station to fill up for the trip. We had to get all of the right music for a long trip like that. That was any dope dealer's wish in the game. We started out playing a good mix tape and reminiscing about all the fun we used to have on the old block.

We made good time because as soon as we got close to our destination, the police pulled us over. I kept a stack of money in a brown paper bag in the car. I learned that from an old hustler who used to travel the highway all the time. I was two steps ahead of the police and had about five hundred dollars in my pocket for expenses. They searched the car for about a hour and couldn't find anything but a marijuana roach. I joked, "Can't a black man get high anymore?" That brought a red flag to my attention so I asked B-Nice to call his cousin and alert him what had just happened; I knew they would be watching us the entire trip. I wanted to turn around but, we had come too far to retreat now.

We arrived to our destination to check in the hotel, but all the hotels said we would have to pay for a hotel for five hours at seventy dollars. I decided to go across the other side of town, where the truckers got their rooms. We got a room for two days, put the luggage in the room, and relaxed while B-Nice called his cousin to let him know we'd made it safely. B-Nice's cousin knew a lot of people, so he was going to find out what was going on with that stop from the police earlier that day. He told us enjoy the city, go shopping, and make sure we got some good pizza while we were there. He would call us when he is ready to put me on to some real business. We found some nice deals and some good Italian food. We spent a lot of time sightseeing because this town was very nice. I really wanted to go closer to the water at night time, to see the beautiful views. We grabbed some food to take back to the room because everybody was getting tired and wanted to enjoy the tub. While B-Nice and I got freshened up and tried on our clothes, his cousin called and wanted us to meet him in a different town. I knew we were in trouble, but B-Nice said he knew where he was going. We made the wrong turn and ended up in a different town. I looked in the rearview mirror and noticed a police was following us for a block or two. He finally pulled us over and said we seemed like we were lost. Then he said that I looked like a drug dealer. I had never seen Lexus go off on the police like that. She almost went to jail, and we had to calm her down. She was about to punch the police and cursed him out. We stayed there for a long time; they checked out everybody before we could go anywhere. They finally let us go and directed us in the right direction to get us back on track. We arrived at B-Nice's cousin's house just in time. I said that B-Nice took us on a wild goose chase. I noticed that when we got in the house, everyone was glad to see B-Nice. They had the kitchen smelling good with Jamaican food. We finally got settled in and greeted everyone with open arms. Then B-Nice's cousin asked me and B-Nice to come in the back room so that we could get our plan together. He told me we would have to leave at different time because the cops were watching us. He was from a strong family who was connected to streets about information.. When I heard that, I knew I was with the right people. It was a dope dealer's dream.

I told his cousin how much money I had. He wanted us to ride with him. I asked Lexus, "Will you be okay until we get back?" We took a couple different turns so he could show us the city. We arrived at this huge, beautiful house with about four big pit bulls guarding it. We were introduced to one of the biggest dope dealers in the world. I was kind of nervous at first because there were some serious people standing in front of the house with guns. He offered us something to drink and explained that the police were watching, so we needed to do everything as planned if we wanted to make it out of his town safely. He took us into a small room and showed us different colors of cocaine. I thought B-Nice was joking, but his cousin told the truth. He asked, "What color do you like?"

I replied, "I need to take back the best to make a statement."

He liked our attitudes, so he said, "Every time you buy, I will front you the rest."

I couldn't wait to get back to my hometown and make a ton of money. We shook the guy's hand and he made a final statement.

"Keep it real with me, and I will keep it real with you." I already had everything planned when I got back to home base. I was making his money first and keeping him straight. This was a major connection. He was a very powerful man, so I knew it would be very easy for him to find me in a small town if I didn't pay his money.

We finally arrived back at B-Nice's aunt's house and were ready to eat. Lexus had entertained everyone so well that his aunt didn't want her to leave, but I had to get back to see what this cocaine was like. We said our good-byes and thanked B-Nice's aunt and cousin for everything; we had really enjoyed ourselves. We went back to the hotel and got some rest for the long drive ahead. B-Nice's cousins were going to call us about when to hit the highway, when all of the cops were changing shifts. He told us he was on his way to put the dope in the right place in the car so that the dogs could not smell it if we did get stopped. We drove carefully with no mistakes going out of the town, because the police were watching for out-of-state tags all day. We made a couple of stops to get snacks and gas. I wanted to stop at the next city over to get some blue crabs, but I knew I couldn't take chances with all this dope on me. People would rob anybody from out of town.

We made it back safely to my hometown. It was strange—as soon as I passed the sign, the whole axel on the car off after hitting all of those potholes in B-Nice's cousin's hometown. They had some bad roads, especially when one was speeding to avoid traffic. I couldn't leave the car—my life was in there, put away. I called a tow truck whose drive I'd known for a long time. I rode with him and called a cab for Lexus and B-Nice. We went to the nearest shop in the area. I had to pay $350 to get it fixed. They finished on time that day, so we went straight to my mom's house. I took B-Nice to the back of the house and told him, "This will be enough dope to keep you straight until I get with you later. Here is some money to go get us two rooms—tonight we are going to celebrate." I thanked him so much for putting me in touch with some real people. I put everything up and took a piece around the corner to one of the biggest dope houses in town. I saw one of my main men, Black Stallion, another hustler that would stay up all night. I asked him to go test this out and added, "The other piece is yours because I haven't seen you in a while." I also gave the whole house some because I was a good-hearted person. I was standing in the living and talking to my man Snake when I heard Black Stallion hit it he said it was the best he'd had in ten years. He ran right through the front door and knocked the whole door down—that was how powerful the dope was. Everyone said, "You've got the best in town. You'd better not go out of town with that!"

Lexus and I could shop for everything we wanted. I finally had a winner after all the years of hustling. Life was grand, and I could buy anything for my family. I met up with Hustleman, got the money, and gave him the new stuff. When he hit it, I thought his eyes were going to pop out of his head. He backed up and said, "Now that is that premium, for real." B-Nice ran the west side, and hustler and I had the south side of town. I didn't have to stay on the streets long because they had everything under control.

As soon I made the dealer's money, I sent it to him. He sent me a letter back and said, "You are a good man. When you finish, come see me—you can get anything you want."

I called B-Nice to meet me at the sub shop and bring me the key to the room; we'd get some of the best subs in town while we were there. B-Nice said, "I will meet you later with a stack of money, dawg." I noticed there was a couple of cars following me as I was going to the room. I never carried too much money on me, but I always had my nine millimeter ready to blast off. I was glad I didn't have Lexus with me, because I would've shot somebody. As I entered the room, someone knocked on the door and announced himself as the housekeeper. It seemed strange— why was the housekeeper still working late? I proceed to open the door, the housekeeper stepped in, and then I saw a foot blocking the door. I pulled my gun out and got it ready. Three guys came to the door and yelled, "Give me the money, and no one will get hurt." I couldn't resist and was robbed at gunpoint. The dealing game was a trip. I didn't even have time to count my money. It was a sign, anyway. I was getting tired of the game because the more money I had, the more problems occurred.

I called Lexus and told her what happened, and she said, "Meet me at your mom's house right now."

We talked a while, and I told her, "I still had a lot of money left after I paid off the dealer. I would love to move to out of town with you and start over with a new life." She agreed and was ready … but I couldn't leave the game alone. I called Hustleman and B-Nice, telling them to keep knocking that work off quickly. I didn't want to tell B-Nice because he was always ready to shoot anybody. I decided to hustle the streets a little bit longer.

One day I decided to sit down with my mom and talk about changing my life. She replied, "I will be praying for you when I go to church today."

I called Lexus back and told her, "I'm ready to meet your mom, because I am ready to slow down. The streets are burning me out."

Her mom agreed to meet me anytime. When we saw each other, we talked about the Bible. We became real close, and she would teach me more about the Bible and how to be a responsible man. I would go to church with them every Sunday and then go to work afterward. I enjoyed listening to the pastor speak on different messages every Sunday. I would go pray every Sunday because I knew I still had a lot of street in me. I was very focused on changing my life around.

I thought about applying at the university in our town and playing on the football team the next season. I talked to her uncle about it. He said, "You still look like you are in shape." I didn't do it because I wanted to get close to God.

I remember one day I was talking to Lexus's mom about moving in to get away from the street life, but she always believed we had to be married first to have sex in her house. I moved everything in the house and brought my new car I had bought with money from hustling. I was free from the street life and was learning more how to be an honest person. I knew I had to get some kind of income coming into the house, so I decided to put in a couple of applications to different organizations. I got a call from a grocery store, and they hired me, so I was working two jobs. I worked grocery third shift, and my other job was second shift. It wasn't what I was used to making in the game, but I grew to appreciate the little things that came my way. Lexus had a little girl name Micah at this time, so every time I would get paid, all of us would go shopping or eat at a good restaurant. We were like a family. Her daughter was a quiet little girl; every time I would come in the house, she would be hiding behind the refrigerator and peeping out at me. She was a very shy and respectable little girl.

I worked the two jobs for almost two years. I started attending church more, getting to know God, and doing more listening in Bible study. The pastor and I became close; she would tell me, "You are a special young man no matter what happens in your life. God has your back." At that time I didn't know what she was saying because there was no love in the streets. Every time I came to church, she would want me pray before I left. One day she asked me and Lexus to come to the back, and she asked us what we had planned for the future. We told her we loved each other and were thinking about getting married. She explained how it was important to understand the future of being married. We went to the park with the pastor after the session and finished talking about marriage. I agreed, and we talked to her mom about it. She agreed and gave us her best wishes. Her mom said, "You can't continue to stay under my roof, not unless you are married."

I talked to my mom about the situation and about getting married. She said, "If you are happy, do what is best for you." That's why I love my mom—she is very understanding and humble about every situation.

Lexus and I got married on a special day at the church where she had been a member all her life. It was a nice wedding, very formal and sweet. After the wedding we went straight to the beach for the honeymoon and had a good time. We walked the beach holding hands and enjoying the sunset. I watched her beautiful smile as the glare from the sunset bounced off her beautiful face. The next day we decided to go get some good seafood from an awesome place. I loved every moment of it because it was good for me to get away. We decided to go shopping at the mall, and the stores had a lot of good deals. We arrived back to our hometown with the reality of being married.

I continued to work two jobs to maintain the little bit we did have at the time. Lexus decided to go back to school to get into the nursing field, and she started working two jobs. We were getting our money together to get our own place.

I was just getting off of my third shift, and when I pulled in the drive way, I noticed Lexus and her mom were arguing. Her mom said, "You and your husband get out of my house!" That was the first time I realized that I had to become a real man. We grabbed everything and put it in our cars. We drove to the nearest hotel to decide what we were going to do next. When we got settled in, we decided to say a long prayer for our future. We talked our situation over for a day or two. We had some money saved to put down on a place, but at the place where we were trying to stay, they were checking everything closely—especially my background. We found a place in the country that was nice and quiet, but we needed more money. I decided to go back to the streets. Lexus didn't want me to, because if something happened to me she had no one to depend on at the time. I told her I would do this differently; I would not go to the city much and deal mostly in the country. I called one of my old friends with the weight to meet me at our old spot. I did everything different this time because I didn't want Lexus involved with the drug game. I tried to spend as much time with her because she was young and new to the game. The street would bring a good girl into the game and make her a bad girl.

We lived in the hotel for a while until our place got put together. We finally moved in and started decorating the house. We continued to work and keep our paycheck coming into our savings. I became well-known in the neighborhood, and so I started supplying everyone that was looking for weight. It became so sweet that I would only see police officers one time patrolling the area. My friend with the weight was giving me anything I wanted, and it was lovely. When my friend would come over, she would bring my main man Burt, another homie from back in the days. I started my own tree business and detailed cars to keep the police off of me. Lexus shopped every day. We bought our first living room and bedroom sets for the house. She was so happy to have her own place, and she wanted to have sex every night. That made me hustle even harder in the streets.

Lexus became pregnant during this time. I had to watch her more and take care of her every need. I decided to buy a landscaping business from a friend of mine who was going through some hard times. Everything was looking good, and we didn't have to worry about bills not getting paid on time. I had everything and decided to quit my jobs. She invited her mom over for dinner, and the first question she asked was how we could afford all of the things in the house. That was one of the biggest mistakes Lexus could have made, to invite her mom while I was dealing drugs. I was hoping she was going to wait a little longer, until I saved about thirty thousand dollars for the future. The Bible says your family can be your worst enemy no matter the situation.

I started noticing a lot more police when a new crowd moved across the street. They were young and full of energy. I would stay up all night long to watch any crazy moves from the police. I called my homebody Weightman and asked him what he had planned today. He was coming out my way to do something, and I asked him to stop by and load me up for the week. When he came to the house, he looked around and said, "Boy, you are doing well. I'm loving the decoration of the house." I told him Lexus picked out everything in the house, but I might be moving because this crowd across the street was bringing the heat. He told me to keep him informed.

I decided to ride though my hometown, because it was a beautiful day. I saw my cousin Dopeman hanging on the block. He didn't ask questions and just jumped in the car, saying, "I'm going wherever you are going. At the time Weightman and I had some nice rides. I took Dopeman to my house because Lexus had been asking about him. He knew I was doing well, but not that well. As soon as we arrived at my house, he wanted some dope to take back to town. He stayed with me a couple of days and met a young girl across the street. Dopeman got the whole house across the street in order. There wasn't a lot of noise anymore, and that made me stay a little longer because the police didn't come around anymore. I took Dopeman back, and then Lexus and I still looked around for a new place. We found something with more peace and quiet, because she was pregnant and needed to be comfortable with the baby. We decided to move to a small town that was building a lot of new houses. We moved in a month later.

I was still hustling, but I needed a job out there because it was a good neighborhood. I applied at a computer company, got the job, and found out that a lot of my old friends worked out there. The pay was good, and I met some new friends who were very cool. One of my old friends, whom I knew through my cousin, was Caleb, and we became hanging partners throughout our journey at the computer company. One night we went out with this guy name Ervin. He drove his van, so Caleb and I, along with Big Daddy and a couple of girls, were in the van getting drunk. Ervin had a nice van; it was custom made with TVs and everything. We decided to go to the park and drink a couple of beers; we bought a lot of beer to last all night. Then Big Daddy wanted to get some liquor, so we went to the liquor store and got some powerful stuff. I had never in my life heard of the alcohol he bought. I found out what it was that night. Caleb and I started drinking it first, straight from the bottle. I was so drunk that I ran out of the van and to a dumpster, jumped up, and threw up in the can. That was the talk of the computer company for a whole month—every time people looked at me, they would start laughing. We had a good time that night. One of the girls liked me and wanted me to go home with her. I told her I was married and that my wife was pregnant, so I needed to get home to check on her. Caleb and I made it a twice a month thing, to reminisce about the old days.

I was still hustling, but I didn't let Caleb know what I was doing because in the game, you don't let outsiders know your business; they can use it against you for leverage in the future. Caleb would come over to watch the football games with me on Sundays. I was sitting back and thinking Caleb was a good guy. Lexus had friend named Angela who was a businesswoman, and she and Caled would make a good couple. I checked on Lexus and asked her whether her friend had a boyfriend. She stated not at that time. I invited both of them to a cookout, and they connected right then. They eventually got married and had three beautiful kids.

The next couple of months went on smoothly, and Lexus finally went into labor. I had packed everything up in my car, which at the time was small. I got on the highway going ninety-five miles per hour down the highway, and a police officer showed me the way. Lexus said, "I think my water busted." I really hit the pedal to the floor. I entered the hospital in the front, and the nurses were waiting for me. They knew Lexus because she worked at the hospital. At the end of the night, we had an eight-pound, six-ounce little boy name Jamie. This was the first time I really had sat down and held a baby without thinking about the streets. I would hold my baby all the time until he went to sleep. Lexus had a friend named Karen who was very supportive, and she would bring us anything we needed for the baby. She was a true friend to Lexus. I loved to see Karen come over and make me laugh all the time; she had a great sense of humor.

I gradually got away from the game and started working full-time at the computer company. I would only serve special people who would call me for dope. I also had to help out around the house. I noticed that after Lexus had the baby, she wanted to start hanging out at the club more. It was cool with me because I wanted to get to know my son. I didn't want my son to grow up like I did, without knowing my dad—I wasn't going to make the same mistake. I did make one mistake, though. I got a call from an old friend, and he was looking for some major weight. I felt that something wasn't right, but I went anyway. Every time I would go into town, something would go wrong. Lexus stayed home with the baby, and I kissed my little man on the head before I left. As soon as I arrived in the projects and made the turn, the police surrounded my car. They got me for a possession charge, took my car, and put me under a twenty-thousand-dollar bond. I had to call my cousin, the bail bond, to come get me out. When I got out I had to argue with Lexus about the stupid move I'd made. After the incident happened, we started arguing everyday about anything and everything. I decided to move out to my mom's house until I got everything back together. I did not like a lot of arguing in a relationship because it would drive me to my grave quicker. I didn't want to leave my son because that was my heart, and I was just getting a bond with him.

My mom welcomed me in with open arms, to give me a little peace and to decide what my next move would be. I started my own business detailing cars to make some honest money. Lexus would bring my son over to let me keep him on the weekends. I enjoyed every minute with my son. My case in court kept getting put off for another day until they received all of the evidence. Lexus and I talked everything out because we had a boy together. She would come over on the weekends and spend the night with me; we would play with our son together. We would have sex on the regular basis, and then she became pregnant with our second son.

My mom was glad that I had moved in with her to help out with my aunt from the city. Her name was Aunt Lou, and she was a sweet woman, although she loved Stars Wars and would eat enough for two grown men. My mom stayed close to the dope spot, so I decided to make some side money in the dope game. This was the time I lost a true friend that I played football with and grew up with; his name was Darryl. He was killed right around the corner from my mom's house. Every time he would see me, the only thing he would do was laugh before he spoke. He used to bring up his hit on me in football, when I was the quarterback. He'd hit me so hard that my shoulders were stuck in the ground.

I was doing well in the dope game until I saw an old friend named Joseph, who use to hustler for me on the block back in the days. I gave him some work, and he acted correctly all of the time … until he got comfortable and decided not to pay me my five hundred dollars, and I had to take care of the situation. The street code is to not let anyone take anything from you, because when they see your soft spot, they will take advantage of the opportunity. I started beating him on top of my truck. As I was beating him, I noticed Lexus and her mom pull up, and they asked me what I was doing. I replied, "He owes me some money. He will not take food out of my kid's mouth." They drove off quickly, shaking their heads in disbelief. They saved him because I was going to bet the black off of him.

My mom found out and decided to move from that area. She was already looking for a bigger place to better accommodate my aunt. My mom has always been the type to take care of other before she takes care of herself. She is a true woman of Christ. My mom found a place near the mall. I was glad when she made that decision because the mall was the best place in town to relax and get away from the drama. No matter what the situation was, Lexus would still bring my son over and give me the report on my second son.

I got a job close to the house, at a car lot. My duty was to report to the boss and see what he had going on for that day. If nothing was happening, I would help Eddie in the back, detailing cars. I learned a lot from Eddie, and he showed me how to really detail a car, including buffing the outside and redoing the carpet in the inside. I thanked Eddie every day for giving me a trade so that I could take it anywhere in the world. Eddie was dedicated to his job; he would drive ten miles every day to and from work.

My stepdad started getting really sick and then died a couple months later. I remember we were at the hospital, and my mom was crying. That was the first time I saw her cry. She is a strong black woman. I had to be there for my mom, because she had always been there for me. At this moment she needed the whole family because no matter what they went through in their marriage, it was still her husband. We had a nice funeral for him, and my mom eventually came back to herself after a couple of months. As everything was getting back together, my aunt died a couple months later. It was a crazy year for my mom and the family.

I continued to work at the car lot with Eddie and the boys; they were like a family to me. Lexus called me one day and said had to go to the hospital because she was about to have my second son. We were in a small town at a car auction, picking up about twenty cars to be shipped back to the car lot. We rushed back to my hometown, but she'd already had my little man. She told me he was a blessing because the cord had wrapped around his throat. They got him out just in time. His name was Deshawn, and he was also eight pounds. The boss and the crew heard about my baby and bought my baby enough supplies to last for a year. I loved working there because everybody was down to earth.

I knew it was time to make a decision—with two boys in this world, it time to get my act together. The next day I decided to have a long talk with the boss about buying my own house. He said he know some people to make this happen. I called Lexus to come look at a couple of places and to find one she would like. We finally got approved for the house, and we decided to make this relationship work one more time. We went talked to pastor about the situation, and we started out doing well. We would take turns feeding the kids. I would always tell her, "We are a family now, trying to build a strong relationship. We have to separate from our parents and build our own family." I learned when I had family too involved in my business, the marriage would not work. It didn't change anything. When we would get on the right track, her friend would come along, and then they would start hanging out to the clubs again. I was being the serious one. I had these boys now and didn't want to be involved with hanging out with friends right now. I didn't go to clubs—I was in the house, safe with my boys. It was okay to go out every now and then to relieve some stress, but not every weekend when we had a lot of responsibility. Lexus and I started arguing again, and she decided to move back with her mom. It was cool with me because like I said, I couldn't do a lot of arguing due to my high blood pressure. I wanted to live a little longer in life. I continued to pay bills at the house and work at the car lot. I couldn't keep the house up with bills by myself, so I decided to rent it out to a couple who had three kids.

I decided to have a party before I would turn the house over to them. and I told all of my friends to come. It was a nice gathering with a lot of women and guys there. I was in the living room talking to three women when I heard a huge bang coming from the back door. Lexus came in through the back door and started swinging at the three girls. The three girls started fighting back to protect themselves; they didn't know what was going on at the time. The party was still a success after that.

The next day my friend T-Bone decided to help me move everything to my mom's house so that I could get ready for the couple to move in the following week. T-Bone was a good friend whom I had met through his brother. We became real cool and hung out every day in the country. T-Bone got in a little trouble with the police; he had a shootout with them and hit one officer in the shoulder. However, he was a real trooper when he was with me. I miss my buddy—he was down for anything.

The following week the couple moved in my place. They paid rent on time for a while, until her husband got caught on a job and immigration sent him back to his country. She had to move out, and I decided to let the mortgage company take the house back. I had to stop working at the car lot because I knew my court case was coming up, and I would be leaving for a while. I explained everything to my boss before I left, and he said he would support me all the way.

This situation got me so stressed out that I decided to invite some old friends over from my high schools days. We went to an old girlfriend's house and started drinking some gin and juice, smoking pot, and doing a couple lines of cocaine. The party became so excited that some of us decided to go get a room at the hotel to make this into a weekend party. We stayed in the room, partied, and watched a couple of games on the big TV. We did a couple more lines of cocaine and decided to go to the club downtown, where the university students partied all night long. They knew how to have fun with alcohol! I wanted to have a blast because I would have to go to court Monday morning. I didn't get any sleep that whole weekend.

I woke up and visited my mom before I went to court. I gave her a kiss and a hug. I went to court and waited until the judge was ready to call my case. I didn't want to go in front this judge, but I didn't have enough money to finish paying my lawyer. The judge sentenced me to sixteen to twenty-two in prison. I wasn't worried about the time served—I was more concerned about my mom, but I knew God had her back. The first stop was to be processed through the system with the other inmates.

While I was at this prison, I saw some people I hadn't seen in a very long time. Prison was not a place to successful in life. I had to watch my back all day, every day. In prison people got hurt over some stupid things. I saw some crazy things happen, such as two men kissing in the shower and having sex. I thought, *Can this be true? I'm dreaming, right? You can take a normal shower in prison.* I saw a guy get stabbed in a card game over a honey bun and a pack of cigarettes. I was lifting weight one day, and a guy picked up one of the bars to the weights and hit another guy in the head like it was nothing. It was the newcomer's first time in prison, and he was getting raped because he came in looking scared. The only way newbies didn't get raped was if they had a close friend or family member in the system. There were fights every day on the basketball court over anything. You could go to lunch, sit down at the dinner table, and get a decent meal—and then someone sitting next to you could get stabbed.

I would keep myself busy on the basketball court, in the weight room, or in the library because it was too easy to get involved with stupid people. It was similar to the streets. It was a hard bid for me because I lost my favorite grandma and aunt while I was in prison. I wanted to go to the funerals but couldn't.

I finally finished my time—it was time to go home. I had a different mindset this time because I had seen more in prison this time then the first time. The system was getting worst every year. When I arrived it was exciting because all my family was there to greet me. It was the summer, so it was time to show off all of my hard work from the weight room. My family had a huge cookout for me. I thanked God for letting me make it home, because not everyone did. Prison was life or death, and it would make men out of the survivors.

We had a good time at the cookout and talked about the old days. I was talking to one of my cousins, and this girl walked up to me and asked me, "What are you doing this weekend?" I told her I was trying to find something to do. We got together, went to the movies, and got a room for the weekend. I noticed she keep getting close to me. She commented, "You are so big." I was thinking in the back of my mind, *Wait until we get in the bedroom.* After the movie we went to a nice dinner and took it back to the hotel room. I had bought some nice roses to give to her, and that sparked the moment with her. We made love all weekend, and she didn't want me to leave her sight. Afterward we stayed in touch to hook up sometimes.

I wanted to focus on getting myself back on track and spending some time with my boys. I started hanging out at the library a lot to get some positive atmosphere in my life. I noticed a change in my way of life. I started thinking about how I could become a positive role model to my two wonderful boys. The game still had me because I would see old friends, and they would ask, "When are you coming back, boss? I found a new spot closer to the gym that you could take over, because you have experience. The spot is near the fish place, right next to the railroad. If the police come, we can run through the path."

I was still staying with my mom because I wanted to make sure she was okay, given that a lot of family members had died in a four-year period. I did everything right to stay on the right path. I went to different jobs, and the first thing they would say was, "We can't hire you because you have a felony." When a person gets a felony it is hard to be productive in the society. I tried hard and didn't want to go back to the game. I went home and laid on my bed, crying about a lot of things in life. If I would've done the right things, I could've been successful in sports. I tried hard to stay positive and honest, but I had to go back to the street where I knew I could make a thousand dollars a day. I decided to get my old crew back together—everyone I grew up with in the projects. They knew the area very well; when something went down, we would know which way to turn. I approached the best hustler on that side of the town, who knew everything about the area, and we agreed how much everybody would get paid on each package. It was great to see the projects crew in action, especially with the best two hustlers on the same field. I had to have the best connections to keep me supplied because this crew could really move the dope. I had two of the top dealers on speed dial to keep me straight. I thought about B-Nice's family during the time. If I had his number, I could've had enough for a year. We had the projects jumping day and night. It was like all of the old customers from cross-town had heard we had the best in town, and they would make a special trip to see me. We had three crack houses, a poker house, and three girls who would take the dope to the customers for me and have sex with them. I was also a pimp in the game. I could help it—all of the fame came at one time when one had a good team. The girls would bring all of my money back, and I would pay them with a bonus. I had a good heart in the game, and that's why every time I would get in the game, I could take over anywhere in my hometown. I always kept Killer around me no matter where I went. I would sit back, eat my fish sandwich, and watch Dopeman, Cool C, and Hustleman take over the streets, running down cars like they were on a football field. I had money stacking up in a week's time.

For some reason Lexus could find me if I was on the moon. Lexus came out of nowhere while I was in the fish spot playing pool and eating a good sandwich and a shrimp plate. She said, "I need some money because I heard you are rolling all the way in my town." That's what I hated about the street people: they talked too much. It was cool because I wanted to get some things for my boys. I gave her five hundred dollars to buy some things, and I asked her when I could see the boys so that I could take them to get some ice cream and go to the park. She said, "Can you help me get this place on the other side of town?"

I said, "Of course, because you have my seed."

She asked me, "Do you want to move in with me, help out with the boys, and get your bond back?"

This would help me stay out of sight on the street as long as I kept them supplied, but it was sometimes important to keep an eye on every activity. I did both in a timely manner. The only day I didn't sell drugs was on Sunday, because that was the Lord's day. When you are selling weight, you have to hustle every day. I had stay close to the block to keep the boys supplied. I also noticed I had a love for the streets because every night was exciting, and one never knew what was going to happen on the block. People would get mad over a small piece of crack and shoot or stab each other. It would be a challenge when the police and the jump-out boys would come through and rob people over small money. I would never keep a lot money on me because I didn't want anybody to get kill. We had a special crew for that situation, whenever people would try something. The younger crowds who hadn't experienced the block would come through with their four wheelers and spark the block up. I couldn't get understand how the big dope dealer couldn't find me, but the kids in the neighborhood would see an ice cream truck, and they would find me and make me buy the whole neighborhood ice cream. I would tell them, "Just bring me back three nutty buddies."

My mom always told me, "Show respect to older people no matter what you are doing in life." I would stop on the porch and ask the older people if they needed anything from the store. They would give me a list, and I would do the shopping myself. They would always give me some good advice about life. When one gets that old, wisdom is like having a million dollars in one's pocket.

I would always go to my cousin Marlo's house to see what he was getting into that night. He would always kick back some wisdom to me about the streets. I decided to change the game up because the business was doing so well. I would give every customer who came to me a special: buy two and get one free. That set a fire alert to the whole town. The deal brought more people to the yard. It got so crazy that people who put their money together would try to stab each other over the extra crack. We were averaging about eight thousand dollars a week with different flips. When the word got out, other dope dealers from across town began coming to our spot. They didn't last a week—the crew made sure of that. My cousin Tootiewas another awesome hustler because she was smart and quick on her feet. Hustleman and Tootiewere dating at the time. It was a great connection, and they never worried about anything. She would always look out for her family first.

I used to love when the boosters with clothes would come through, especially Stephanie. She would look out for and would get my boys' sizes, and carrying almost everything in the store. The business was doing so well that I decided to get Lexus some furniture in the house to make the kids be comfortable. She also got a bedroom outfit to make herself comfortable. It was a great year to have things in life, but every good thing comes to an end. I used to sit back and watch the guys who used to drink that wine all day under a shade tree and talk junk, and sometimes a fight would break out. The shady tree mechanic would be next to these guys working on different cars in the neighborhood. I finally realized I was in deep again because everyone needed me to keep the block supplied with dope. I would never let anyone know where I lived, except Hustleman, Cool C, and Dopeman. If something went down, I would know who was telling the police because I had ears everywhere. When one had money, it would move a mountain. I also noticed the block was getting hot because the police would ride around all day for a couple of weeks. When they did that, they were getting ready to do a major bust. I noticed a couple of new cars would ride by at night, so I would put more people on each corner just in case they wanted to do a drive-by and shoot someone. We would get them before they would get out of the neighborhood. It was getting so crazy that I decided to go across the railroad tracks for a couple of days to visit the hustler Mary's sister and her kids. I would give them some money every time I saw them. Mary was like a sister to me, and we grew up in the projects together. I was close to her sister, too, who would see me and stay on me about school every time. She stayed in the projects about a mile from my neighborhood, and there was also a lot of money out there. If someone wanted something to smoke, she would call me to come back to the projects. Sometimes I would bring the crew and stay over to drink alcohol, smoke weed, and play spades.

I would take a special trip to visit Pat and her daughter, Meeker, who stayed on a different street from Mary. They would tell me the street life is a dead-end for a hustler. Every time they would see me, Pat would put me in a headlock, and her daughter would punch me in the stomach. They were like family to me. When I got deep into the game, I decided to go back when it got dark because I didn't know who was riding in those cars from earlier. I never forgot about the incident when some guys jumped out on me and robbed me for a half ounce of cocaine. I continued to be careful about any strange cars coming through the block.

We had fun with cookouts for the neighborhood on beautiful days. We would play craps and dominos for money. I decided to go home later and see how my boys were doing at the house. While I was at the house, my nephew Cassidy decided to come over and play against me in the Madden football game. He would go to my refrigerator, grab a huge plate of sandwiches, and then ask me, "Do you want one, Uncle Malik?" I can give it to him: he made the best sandwich a person could want while watching a game. He could never beat me in Madden football. When he decided to go home, I took my boys to the mall to get some more games. It was great to spend time with my boys.

I had to go back to the block because the boys had finished everything. Lexus and I decided to get a room to get away from everybody. Lexus was told me, "Don't go tonight—do it tomorrow." I went over to drop the different packages off to Hustleman, Dopeman, Cool C, and the rest of the crew. I got a phone call from my homie at the hotel who wanted some weight. I took an ounce and a half and pulled up at the hotel to serve him the ounce, and he went right to the undercover and gave him some drugs. I tried to tell that nut it was the police. I backed the car up and got out of the parking lot. The police were right behind me in a unmarked car. I had to get my drugs in the right place to get them out the window. I went down the avenue going ninety-five and swerving around traffic. I made it to the intersection of the two lanes and hit another car. I jumped out of the car and took off running toward the hotel where Lexus was staying. I leaped a fence with the dope in my hands and landed perfectly. I put the dope in a good hidden place. The cops were still trying to surround me, and this big guy was running behind me and said, "Damn, you can run for a big guy." They finally got me and took me to jail. The big guy made sure he put me in his car because he talked to me all the way to jail. He said, "You need to be playing football for somebody."

I said, "I'm too old, and I have a criminal record now."

They took me to jail and charged me with hit and run, resisting arrest, and drug paraphernalia of a blunt in the car. They put me under a ten-thousand-dollar bond.

I got out and went straight to the room. I told Lexus what happened, and she said she had seen it on the news. She said, "You'd think you are in a movie or something." When I went to court for the charges, they looked at my past and gave me eighteen to twenty-two months to serve in prison. I went to a small town first to do my process methods. I saw a lot of my school friends in the yards. We lifted weights together and talked about the old days. It was good to reunite with friends and family, but not in prison. I remember they had a weightlifting competition, and this guy name T-Max had been in prison for about ten years. He was the strongest person in the whole camp. I realized a lot of people were scared of him because he was big. All of my friends asked me to compete in the weightlifting competition. I agreed because I didn't want to let my hometown down. I worked out harder every day because after being on the streets, I didn't have a chance to work out on the regular basics.

It was competition day, and all of my friends was bragging and betting on me to bet him. It was like a heavyweight fight. I came out first to do my part, and he beat me by fifty pounds on the bench lift. He had the upper hand from the beginning, and it came down to the squats with our legs. I knew my legs were more powerful because I had been working on my legs for fifteen years. He went first and squatted about 550 pounds. I was impressed to see him do that. I warmed up with my hometown cheering for me. I told the judges to put 650 pounds on the bar. It was the only way I would be him and make a statement to his people: "Don't mess with my hometown." I won the competition and received the trophy with honors. When I walked on the camp, I had respect from the inmates and the guards. The women guards would hold a conversation with me every day and ask me, "Are you going to try to play football or something when you get out? You have a lot of talent." It was sad to leave there—after all, it was only a process camp. I exchanged numbers with all of my friends. I left that night and was on my way to a tough prison where everybody was doing hard time.

When I arrived, I saw the one person I had been wanting to see for a long time. I knew he had been down for about twenty years for raping an old lady. I wanted to get my hands on him so bad because he used to beat on me when I was twelve years old. He was the neighborhood bully and the snitch to the police. They shipped him the next day because I put the word out on the yard through a friend to let me get my hands on him. They gave me my supplies and took me to my room, where I saw an old friend I hadn't seen in about ten years, J-Rock. I used to date his sister back in the day. He was glad to see me, and we would hang out and talk about the fun we had on my old block. He was in a different area, so we couldn't see each other that much. When we did get to see each other, we would meet in the yard, walk the track, or play basketball.

In prison I had to be careful on that basketball court and while lifting weights, because I saw a lot of bad things happen on both. I wanted to get in on the basketball tournament where outsiders came to see us play on the weekends. We would play different section in the building. I was on team with this guy named "Why Me." He was in prison for a long time, so he didn't care about winning or losing. He would get mad at me because I could take over a game with my size. The boys in prison gave me a nickname, LJ, because my game was so nice. We would argue after every game. Everybody else was mad at him, but I never backed down from another man. J-Rock broke it down to him; I didn't hear anything else out of him anymore.

I would hit the weight room harder every day because I wanted to look good when I came home and a lot of these guys in prison had life sentences, so I would have to protect myself. I was benching a lot of weight, and this white guy name Henry asked to work out with me. He wanted me to train him every day. He was a hard worker, and he started to open up to me about his situation. He would tell me the reason why he was in prison; he would never see the other side unless he was going to another prison. He was a very spiritual person and loved the Lord. He told me he got two life sentences and sixty years. I wanted to stop working out with him right then, but I could learn something from his mistake, and so I learned more about the Lord. He invited me to his room later so we could read some scriptures, and then he would tell me the reason why he was incarcerated.

After dinner and a shower, I got dressed and went to visit Henry. I couldn't sit right in the room—the rule was sit by the door at night, because the guards couldn't see what was going on in the room. Henry was a very spiritual brother and believed the Lord would forgive him for all of his mistakes. He knew it was getting late so he decided to tell me the reason why he was in prison. He said he had caught his girlfriend cheating on him with another guy while they were still dating. He killed the guy and then dragged his girlfriend in the living room, where the rest of family was having a family gathering. He killed the father, mother, grandmother, sister, cousins, and two babies. He grabbed her, took her outside, and attached her to the back of a lawnmower and dragged her around the whole town until she came apart. Then he buried her head. My first thought was to get up and never see him again, but I knew God had changed him, so I had to be there as a friend. We became really close and read together every night. He was really smart with the Bible and would break everything down for me to get a better understanding. When I left his room every night, I felt like a wise man. When he had come into the system, he was cutting people and almost killed three inmates, but he found the Lord one day while talking to an old man named Outlaw, who had been in prison for forty years before Henry had arrived.

The next day I was leaving to go to another camp, and Henry said one thing to me that stuck with me. He said, "Malik, you have a second chance in life. I will never get a second chance until I see Jesus. No matter what, do something with your life, and especially for your kids." He wanted me to take advantage of my second chance. I gave him a hug and told him I would never forget him. The next day they shipped me off to green clothes honor; when you got there, the next step was home. I was on the bus thinking about I wished Henry and J-Rock could come with me and celebrate with me, and I thought about what I'd do for them and my kids. When I was at the other prison camp, it was just like being on the block in my hometown. I was going home with the thought to do better in life. I wanted to make a change in someone's life so that they wouldn't make the same mistake Henry and I made throughout our journeys.

When I was at the other camp I was selling Black and Milds to survive through the rest of my time. I would get Lexus to meet me wherever I would go to work. She gave them to me, and we would have sex every time. It was a relief to have that after a couple of years.

I saw a lot of strange things in the prison system. I didn't involve myself because I thought about what Henry had told me. I thought, *When I get out this time, I will make a change in people's lives.* I took some picture with some of my homies before I left. I had a long talk with my homeboy C-Lo because he was a loose cannon in prison and would fight on command. He had my back all the way, and he reminded me of B-Nice on the streets.

I got out of prison a free man, and I didn't look back. Lexus picked me up in red lingerie. I wanted to pull the car over as soon we got down the highway. I was so excited to see her even though I'd heard something about her when I was locked up. She didn't think about street talk reaching a prison. I didn't stress it because I had a purpose in life now. We made love for two days. We did it so much that I couldn't feel my body. I was really glad to see my boys; they had gotten bigger and looked good. Lexus seemed like she missed me. All of my family members were happy to see me and welcomed me home with a surprise party. I partied with them for a couple of days. All weekend I visited everybody that wanted to see me.

That Monday I got on the grind to find a job. It was hard because every time I would get close to getting the job, the first thing they would ask me was, "Do you have a felony?" I didn't give up, and finally I landed an electrician's helper job. I wanted this position because I needed to get a trade for the future. I was glad because if I went back to the streets, I would be doing ten or fifteen years the next time I was busted. I worked there for a while until the week after tourism, and everybody got laid off due to a lack of work. I got back on the job search, and it was back to the felony blocking my prospects.

Lexus knew I was getting mad, so she said, "Let me talk to someone I know at a plant across the river." The lady agreed to interview me because of the lady at church who was the crew leader at the plant. Lexus knew this lady personally from church. I went in for the interview and got the job. I enjoyed working there because everybody was making some real money and saving for the future. I would work all the time, especially overtime. I met some real cool people there; we were like a family. Sometimes my car would break down, and Mr. Anthony and Ms. Annette would give me a ride. I want to thank those guys for keeping me focus.

We used to go to Dominick's house and play Madden football when we got off work. It was the first time I didn't think about going to the streets to survive. I worked so much that I finally got a chance to buy a brick house, and Lexus was ready to get it. I used to love going to work, until one day Dominick pulled me to the side and said, "I have some bad news. The plant will be closing and shipping overseas."

In the back of my mind I thought, *Why are we making other countries rich?* My heart dropped because I was trying to save a lot of money in my 401K pension. I came back the next day to see what they had to offer. They had different types of packages for each individual. They had a package where we would could go back to school for two years with pay, or receive benefits from the company with them, matching everyone's 401K pensions. I took the school option because I could get an education with a trade and have income at the same time.

It was time for a vacation because we hadn't been on one in a while. I decided to get my 401K out to take my boys to the beach and have a good time. I was really pissed off at the system, especially when I was really trying to stay away from the streets. I had a good time with my boys, and we played in the ocean and rode bicycles around the beach. We went shopping and got some seafood to take back to the room. We stayed for four days and three nights.

# V. Academic Achievement

When I got back from the beach, I had a lot on my mind. I went straight to college to get my package started as soon as possible. The more I waited around, the more my mind would start thinking about my past. I went to class and met a lot of new faces, but the game was still on my mind. I started thinking about what Henry had told me during our sessions.

I saw Dominick on a regular basis. He was taking electronics classes, which was next door to me. I decided to join the weight room and keep my mind off of negative things. I'm glad I joined because I started a little hustle. Some of the guys didn't know how to work out, and they agreed to pay me to show them how to work out. I did this for a while until they learned on their own. I had a workout partner named Lewis, and I got him in shape in no time. They decided to have a weightlifting competition at the college, and it was a nice idea because a lot of people showed up. I won the competition by benching five hundred pounds. My photo is on the wall right now at college.

I was getting close to graduation, and class was getting harder. I wasn't working, so I decided to ride through the old neighborhood to see what was going on. I saw my cousin Dopeman, he said he wasn't doing well. I didn't like to see him looking like that, so I decided to get some dope. I knew who was selling the major weight, so I saw Hustleman. He said he had a connection, and I asked him, "How do you know him?"

He said, "It's a cousin of our old connection, from back in the days."

I remember because I used to do business with this connection on my old block. I bought an ounce, gave Dopeman some, and bagged the rest up and gave it to Hustleman for some work. I knew in my heart it wasn't the goal I'd set out to accomplish. The thing about the street was that it was a lot of temptation with the flow of money. I hit them off with the dope and continue to go to school to complete my degree.

I didn't know the game had changed, and one of my closest friends was setting me up at the same time. I really put a lot of trust in this individual. I'd heard the rumor before that the one closest to you will be the one who brings you down. Everything was going smoothly until Lexus called me one day and said the police had been following her for two days. I told her she was paranoid. I went through the block and hit everybody off, telling them when they finished, they should give the money to Dopeman. I never forgot what Lexus told me about the police incident. I went to serve one of my long-distance customers, and I noticed there police following me for a couple of miles, but I didn't really pay attention to him because I was focused on the money. I made a lot of money during the day, but when it turned dark I was about to go sell seven grams of coke to a local customer for four hundred dollars. As I was about to make the turn to go to the lady's house, the police surrounded my car. When they approached the car, they knew I was dealing drugs. They found the seven grams in the car and tried to take both Lexus and me to jail. I explained to them that she didn't know what was going on about the drugs. I didn't want her to go to jail because she had to take care of my boys. I knew in my heart I was facing ten years because of all my past experiences. They handcuffed me and took me to jail to get a bond, making it fifty thousand dollars. I had to wait for a while until they dropped the bond a little lower.

While I was in jail, I talked to a lot of old friends about life. I wanted to make a change, but the game had my soul tight. I had the right ideas in my mind, but I had no faith in God. I started to read more and get a better understanding of faith. I decided to go outside one day in the back and try to show the boys that I could still jump and touch the top of the basketball rim. I tried it a couple of times, but the last time I came down and busted my knee. They had to rush me to the hospital and do surgery. When I was in the hospital, my family came to visit me, and Lexus told me they had dropped my bond to where I can get out after the surgery. The surgery went well, but it hurt badly. I made bond and went home with a broken knee. I had to stay in bed for three months and thought, *What else could go wrong? I'm trying to graduate from school. This will be my first degree.*

Lexus and the boys were very supportive throughout my process. Lexus decided to let her dad come and stay with her, to help out around the house. I called my teacher and let him know what had happened, asking whether I could make up the work in bed. Lexus would go out to the school, get all of my assignments, and take them back when I had completed them. When I noticed I could walk normally, I decided to go back to school. My classmates were happy to see me again and almost broke my neck with different kinds of hugs. I waited until I got in the classroom and asked the teacher if I could make an announcement to everyone. I explained to my classmates that I had gotten into some major trouble and might not be able to graduate with them. I had done a lot of bad things in my past, and now it was catching up with me. My teacher and my classmates decided to get in a circle and pray for me. I felt good after the prayer from so many people. I went home from class, gathered everyone in the living room, and explained the situation to my boys. "I might be going away for a while, but in my heart I am going to get a second chance. I want everybody to take care of your mom." They started crying really hard because I was always in and out of their lives. It hurt me badly, and I decided to take a long walk with them to the grocery store so that we could talk about all the fun we'd have. It was a nice walk until I returned to the house and noticed my arm and wrist was bigger than normal. I called the ambulance, and they checked my blood pressure: it read 225 over 185, which was nowhere normal. They decided to rush me to the hospital as quickly as possible because they had announced me over the microphone as dead on arrival. They found something wrong with me that was not normal. When they got to the hospital, they rushed me through the double doors and put me on a table. A lot of people rushed into the room. The doctor came to the conclusion that it must me a blood clot somewhere, for the blood pressure to be that high. They hooked me to a machine, shot dye in me, and found a blood clot next to my heart. They rushed me to the operation table and started doing what they did best. The nurse explained to me, "If this blood clot busts, you will die instantly."

I started talking to this male nurse, and he asked me, "Who is your favorite football team?" I told him the Steelers. As we were talking, they got me ready. I didn't mind the prep talk until I turned around and saw a long needle. I don't remember anything after that step.

When I woke up, they explained to me, "We got the blood clot just in time." When they took me back to my room, they couldn't get me in because everybody was there. My family and classmates had thought that was the end of me. There were so many people that the nurse announced that they couldn't be in here at one time. "We will have scheduled you a visitor list," she said.

When everybody left and I had peace and quiet, I decided to get my Bible out, and I started talking to God. I thanked him for giving me a second chance to see my family. I said, "God, I'm making a promise to you. If you will give me a second chance to see my kids grow up without been locked up, I will never touch another foot in the street life." One can make a promise to an average person and break it, but one cannot make a promise to God and think he will forget it. I got better from all of the medicine, and my family came to visit me on the regular basics. My mom would come so much that they knew her full name.

The doctor sent me home and told me takes it easy for a while. I went back to class to thank everyone for the support, and the teacher said I should stay away from salt and soda. I had a better idea: the gym was free at school, so I decided to work out. I worked out until it was time for me to go to court. I went home and got ready for court the next day. I spent a lot of time with my family that day, and Lexus and I made love the rest of the night.

I got up the next morning with a blessing in the air and had a good country breakfast. I kissed my boys and told them I loved them. I went to court I saw my lawyer and talked to him for a second. He said, "The district attorney is trying to give you the most time they can get out of the judge, around fifteen years. I don't see any hope but prison. You will need a miracle from God."

I knew in my heart God had my back. If it was meant in my plan from him, it was for a reason. I kept my faith from all of the prayers. I noticed time was ticking along before recess. They finally called me up, and my heart dropped. I stood with my head up and took my punishment like a man. It was around 11:30 when they called me up, but the district attorney didn't have all of the paperwork together. The judge said, "We will have a recess until after lunch is back, at 2:00 PM. I hope you have everything together when we come back." He gave me more time to call all of my family to come see for the last time before the sentencing. My mom brought the whole church, and they put me in the center and prayed for me for thirty minutes. My mom treated everybody to lunch for supporting her son. Lexus also came down with my boys.

After recess the judge came back in and called me back up to be sentenced. He stated, "Malik, I don't know what happened to me when I was in my chamber, but something touched me and wanted me to give you a second chance in life. I remember when you were seventeen years old. You had one of the best fastballs in this town. I would rush home to get take a shower, and I wouldn't miss you playing for nothing. I would get you to sign things for me because I knew you were going pro, and I could tell everybody that you'd signed this for me at a young age. I try to tell these young kids with talent that drugs have taken over some good athletes in this town. I have a feeling you are going to do the right thing this time. I'm putting you on probation for 4 years suspected, with 120 months to 134 months."

I looked at my lawyer and said, "God is in this place—can you feel his presence?" I thought about Henry in prison and how I'd also made a promise to him.

The judge said, "When you graduate from school, send me an invitation, and I will come to it. I also want to come to visit sometime and speak to some of these kids in trouble." I thanked the judge and left the courthouse with my family, smiling. God had done his part with two second chances in a couple of months. It was time for me to keep my promise. I told my family to meet me at my mom's house; I had one more thing to do before I started my journey. They thought I was going to do something stupid. As I was riding down the street, I said to myself, *I've never seen a person with the record I have get a second chance like that. I know if they did get a chance, they told the police some information.* I didn't have to use that tactic because I had God on my side.

I pulled up on the block and saw my cousin Dopeman, and I said, "I need to talk to you about something real important, right now." We walked to the green utility box in the projects where I grew up. I told him I was finished with the game. "You and the boys can have everything; just let me get a couple dollars so I can find a job." I went to some of the guys that owed me some money and got some it from them. I collected as much as I could, and then Dopeman and I went back to the green box and started talking and drinking beer, and I smoked one more blunt. I was trying to convince him to change his life from the game. I told him I had to go and walked off. He called me one more time. I said, "What's up?"

He said, "Don't talk about it—be about it." It got me kind of hot because he didn't believe in me, but it didn't matter because I had made a promise to God.

I drove back to my mom's house where all of the church members were waiting to see me. They started calling me the chosen one for God. I told my mom and the church members, "Thanks for everything. I'm about to go see my boys." I hugged them so tightly I that didn't want to let go all day. I had a real second chance to prove to them and me that miracles could happen every day.

I stayed overnight and decided to go to class to thank them for the prayers and support. When I walked in the door, they were looking at me like they seen an angel. I went to class every day and decided to work out more for my health. I was working out so well from that a lot of guys would talk about me around campus. I had a lot of guys come up to me and ask me how much I'd charge to train them. I had about ten guys during the week with different schedules. That was a good side job for me. They say you can take the hustler out of the street, but you can't take the hustle out of the person. I had a workout partner, and he was very excited to get back into the gym. He lost about thirty pounds in no time. He got so into it that I couldn't sleep because he would come to my house and say,

"Get up—can't get nothing done sleeping!" He got his confidence up with every workout. It was some a time at the school.

I finally finished all of my classes, and it was time to graduate. I went home and told Lexus, "When I graduate across the stage, I want to move out of my hometown. If I stay, it will just be more temptation. I have a better chance to get a job in other areas than in my hometown." We went searching on the Internet, and she found a couple of jobs. My felony record made it a little tougher. It turned out I had a couple more classes to complete to graduate, but we decided to go ahead and move anyway. I called an old friend that worked at a hospital. I got Lexus a job at the hospital, and it was great place to work.

We found a nice apartment in the big city, and I decided to let her go ahead and move; I would keep the kids with me until they finished school. I took a couple more classes to get closer to my graduation time. We moved all of the furniture and supplies to the big city, and then the boys and I came back to finish school. We finished everything on time in the summer. We then caught the bus to the city so that Lexus could come pick us up. We went to the apartment to put our luggage in the closet.

I noticed she had been acting strange during the couple of months she was up there; she would argue about small things. I told her I'd just come out of a major surgery, and we were new in the area. She replied, I've met people in the area. I'm not new—you are." I humbled myself because I was trying to be successful in another town. I thought about how I had a better opportunity. I was waiting on a couple of companies from the neighborhood area, but I was still unemployed because I had two more classes to complete. I decided to go to the rest of my classes at a community college out of town. It was a nice program, but it wasn't like my old school. It seemed like the more I would come to the house, the more Lexus would argue. I did not want to do the same thing out of town that we'd done in our hometown. This was a new start for our lives. I already had my mind set on getting my doctoral degree because this was an education area. It didn't last long because she already had her mind made up to let me go.

I remember coming home from community college one day, and I saw the police in the neighborhood. I thought that somebody must have gotten hurt with five police cars in one area. When I stepped to the house, the officer asked me my name. I told them my name, and they said, "Lexus does not want you in the house anymore." It was night, and it had to be twenty degrees outside in the winter.

I couldn't believe this was happening. I begged her, "Don't do this—we can talk it out."

She said, "I found someone else while you were staying in our hometown." She didn't have the nerves to tell me this a couple months ago. I was really upset, but I knew it was for the best because I didn't want to keep arguing in front of the kids. I went in the house and grabbed all of my clothes and supplies. I was really hurt about this situation, but I knew I had God on my side. The police asked me to leave the property after I gave her house key. I grabbed my things, walked to the store, and called my mom. My mom wanted me to jump on the next bus to come back home, but I couldn't go back there. I told her I had God on my side and would be fine. I cried for a while because all I was trying to do was get my education in order to have a better life for my kids. Lexus wanted to destroy that for the younger boy. I took my stuff to the nearest bridge, and I slept there until the next day, when it turned dark again. It was cold, and I had to swallow my pride.

I remembered that a friend of mine always told me, "Never let your pride keep you hungry." I finally realized what he was saying about life. I was always taking the easy way out. It was time to become a man. I stepped in the middle of the street and asked God to direct my path. "I can't go back to hustling because I made a promise to you with a second chance."

I started walking up a hill, and this old man told me to follow him. He took me to the shelter, which meant it was time for me to get my pride right. He introduced to a guy name Mr. Benny, who was a nice guy until one crossed him. I told Mr. Benny I was in school trying to get my bachelor's degree. He said, "I love stuff like that—a young man trying to get his education." He gave me my own room so that I wouldn't have distractions. I stayed there for a long time to save some money. Mr. Benny was cool with any ideas I had. I met some cool people who needed encouraging words from a true brother. I showed some guys how to use the computer to find jobs.

It was still hard to find a job with my record. I didn't know what to think about that situation. You never know where God will put you to touch someone's soul. He needs soldiers who will speak to the unjust as well as the just. I kept going to Durham Tech to finish my English and math courses, so that I could graduate from Pitt Community College. I completed that program, and it was time to complete my bachelor's degree. While I was at the community college, I met this fine young girl name Shontell. She must have seen the hurt in my heart, because she asked me, "Do you need someone to talk to?"

I replied, "Of course I need a friend right now."

She invited me to her house for dinner. When I went to dinner, I met her kids. For some reason they loved to throw things at me. I decided one day play a trick on them. I asked them to meet me outside and said I had a surprise for everyone. I had the water hose already set up, so all I had to do was turn it on. I got them wet, and they thanked me for having such a good time. They became very close to me. They would say, "You are so crazy, you make us laugh."

Shontell and I became close. She would want me to go pick up one of her sons from school because the kid's daddy was always busy. She told her mom about me, and I finally met her. She told Shontell, "You need to marry him soon. He is very handsome, and he has his head on his shoulders." I would spend more time at her house after school before going to the shelter.

I finally got into a major university to go for my bachelor's degree; I would take all my classes online. When I was in class, Shontell would call me and tell me, "I think I will cook your favorite tonight. Can you stop by?" I think she was trying to spoil me. When I came over at night, I noticed she loved to smoke weed. She looked beautiful smoking weed, though I know that is strange to say. She was a beautiful lady and had a fine body. She would smoke her weed, put the kids to bed, and take me upstairs to make love to me all night. She would give me compliments, like "You are handsome, with pretty skin and a nice build." She started playing that old-school music while we made love. I thought I was going to marry her. I had to tell her I was already married. She didn't care. "We will take care of that and get you a divorce quick." We communicated well when it came to the kids. She loved that I thought of her kids every day.

I was also missing my kids. Lexus's new boyfriend had her going out and clubbing so much that she didn't call me to let me know how they were doing.

Shontell and I became so close that we couldn't be apart from each other, but I had to go back to the shelter to keep my spot there. When I arrived at the shelter, Mr. Benny's assistant said, "You must have met someone, because you are smiling ear from ear." He was a cool guy who kept up with everybody business. I went to my room to see if everything was straight. He came up to my room and said, "A lady named Lexus came by to tell you she was sorry, and she wants you to come back home." I wasn't listening to what he was saying—she'd found somebody else, and now I'd found somebody who made me happy. I will never forget, but I will forgive, about the incident of being put out in twenty-degree weather.

I told him, "I have to go to class on campus. I'll see you when I get back." I had a sweet person at the library on campus to help me with my homework. She would call the university to see if I had to get some important information for different classes. I was getting a lot of work done on time and was getting closer to finishing my bachelor's degree. I was so close that I wouldn't give up no matter what situation came my way. I was so focused on school that I sometimes forgot to go see my probation officer. They weren't thinking about me as long I wasn't getting in trouble and I paid my money on time.

I was leaving the probation office one day when I got a phone call from Mr. Benny. I thought it was some bad news. Instead, he told me that an old friend of his wanted me to speak in front of some students about my survival and still going to school to maintain an A average. I agreed to give back to my community.

I finished another semester and was on my break, so I could speak to the students. I spoke to about fifty kids, and they were very impressed with my story. They asked me, "Why don't you write a book and touch the world?"

I replied, "I'm working on it right now." They said they wanted a copy as soon as I finish it. I felt really important and was happy to get some feedback from these intelligent students.

I had it good at the shelter, and the assistant would call me when it was time to eat. When you missed supper, you had go all the way down the street and find a restaurant. There were some good Christian people at the shelter serving the meals. I would always say to myself that would be one of the things I would do if I became successful in life. They made sure they took care of everyone. After everyone ate, they would make a lot of noise, especially if a game was on for the evening. I went to my room to get some rest. As soon as I would lie down, Shontell would call and ask me what I was doing. She would make comments like, "I miss you. I wish you were here." I would tell her that once I took a nap, I would be over.

I was ready to come over because I thought it would be boring at the shelter, but these guys were crazy. They would argue over food, supplies, and more. I was touching some of the guys' lives because some of them found a job and felt good about themselves again. God knows how to put you in the strangest places to do good work. I learned how to swallow my pride and trust in God throughout my journey. I woke up, went to Shontell's house, and had some turkey wings and some good vegetables waiting for me as soon as I got in the door. The kids were excited to see me. After I ate, we went shopping to buy the kids some more school clothes. We had a great time. I noticed Shontell keep pulling me to every jewelry store to look at rings. I thought, *She really does like me.* I stayed the night and went back to the shelter to get ready for class.

While I was coming down the steps, I noticed a new face. He seemed like a wonderful guy, and his name was Greg. He seemed very smart. He asked, "Are you the one everybody talks about? You go to school?" He started going to different classes with me to get the feel of what I was doing in class. We become comfortable around each other. If he knew something about my assignment, he would lead me in the right direction to get the information in the library. He was a smart guy and said he was going back to school. We would take long walks, and he would talk about how disappointing he was to his family. I would buy lunch and anything else, because he was a nice guy. We walked back to the shelter, and I would go upstairs and go to sleep.

The next day I met this guy called Thief. He was a smooth guy and would steal on a regular basis to provide for his needs. I tried to talk to him about the importance of doing different things with his life. I would bring up my prison experiences, but it went in one ear and out the other. While I was talking to Thief, Shontell called; she wanted to see me because she hadn't seen me in a couple of days.

Shontell came with her mom, and I was glad to see her, too. We went to the restaurant where all the celebrities that played basketball for the school ate at on the regular basics. The owner said everybody used to come here every week to get their soul food. We enjoyed our meal, and her mom wanted to know what I had planned for the rest of the evening. "I'm finished with all of homework," I said.

Her mom said, "that's what I'm talking about—an educated brother. I will probably need you this upcoming weekend to help me move all of my stuff from out of town. Can you drive a U-Haul? Can you get someone to help you on this trip?"

I had the perfect guy: Thief. He was not doing anything but taking people things. I called him and asked, "Would you like to take a trip with me to your hometown? I will pay you for the trip." That was all I had to say to him. I told him, "I will pick you up Thursday to stay with me Friday." I stayed with Shontell that whole week because she wanted to be next to me.

I knew I had to get up with Thief early in the morning because otherwise he'd get on that stealing journey and would be hard to find. I ran into him coming out of the store. I jumped out and told him, "It's time to go to your hometown." He went back to the shelter to grab a couple of item to take with him. We drove over to Shontell's house to meet her mom. The U-Haul truck was waiting at the house as soon as we pulled up. We ate breakfast and then got on the highway. Shontell gave me a kiss and told me to be careful; it was raining hard. She wanted to ride with me, but her mom wanted her company.

We drove for a while until we stopped to get some snacks and fill up the truck's gas tank. We got back on the highway, and the traffic was bad, but I got through all of the bad, slippery turns. We arrived at the storage after having a problem going through the tolls. Her mom was thankful that we'd made it safely with the truck. We took a long nap because of the long ride, and Shontell slept in my arms. When we finished loading the truck, we took another long nap and woke up to eat at a cool restaurant. We were about to get back on the road, and Shontell declared, "I'm riding with my baby this time." While I was driving, she was under my arm and close as she could be. We drove back in some heavy rain, so it made it difficult for me to keep the truck between the white lines. She was still close to me and asked me whether everything was okay. The Thief talked to us all the way back.

We drove safely but ran out of gas as soon as we got back in town. We were stuck on the side of the highway. We got everything straight and made it to the nearest gas station. Her mom met us at the gas station and filled the truck up so that we could make it back to the U-Haul place. When we arrived back at the house, we locked all the doors and parked in a good neighborhood. I saw Thief with his hands out, so I paid him for helping me with the trip. He took off running so quickly that I knew he was headed to the dope man. Shontell went with her mom to get the kids. I went upstairs, took a shower, and went straight to bed. I slept like a baby. While I was resting, Shontell was trying to have sex with me. I couldn't turn down that fine body down no matter how tired I was.

The next day I grabbed all of my stuff and headed back to the shelter to start another semester in class. I was on campus every day, getting help to complete my assignments on time. I was still getting unemployment because I hadn't found a job yet. I applied everywhere to seek employment in the town. I called the judge a couple of times to see if I could get my record expunged, because my past was hurting me.

I didn't give up, with the long walks to class and riding the buses all day; I never had a car in the area. One day I was on the bus and saw an old friend from high school; we used to play football together. We talked for a while, but then I had to get to class. I told him, "I think I'd have a better chance getting a job in a different area if I get my education." I finally finished my bachelor's degree, and it was a dream come true. It wasn't easy for me, but I didn't give up on my goal. I wanted to treat myself for my accomplishment, so I decided to go shopping and get a room in another area for a couple of days. I stopped to pay my phone bill first and met a lady from my hometown. We talked for a while, and I think she felt a connecting between us because she invited me over to her house for dinner. She had been at the hospital in the area for a couple of years. She invited some friends over to pay spades after dinner. We enjoyed the night and exchanged numbers before I left.

I called Shontell and asked her, "Can you see if your mom can keep the kids? I want to take you to a different area with me for a couple of days, to eat dinner and go shopping."

She called me back and said, "I'm ready—come get me!"

We went to Triangle Area and got a nice room with a beautiful spa and everything. We shopped all day and found some good restaurants. We were on our way back to her hometown when my mom called and said my favorite cousin was sick in the hospital. I spoke to him for a while and found out he would have to have heart surgery next weekend. He said he wanted to come to this area's hospital to do the surgery. I told him, "If you come out here, I will have a jersey waiting for you at the hospital." He went ahead and had a successful surgery at our hometown hospital, and he went home safely.

When I and Shontell arrived at the house, she was upset about something her mom had said to her, and she took it out on me. We argued for a while about something I never thought she would have said about me. I was very mad and rushed out the door because I needed her support, especially with my favorite cousin sick. I decided to catch the next bus going to the shelter.

I stepped onto the bus, and the bus driver looked at me up and down. She asked me to ride the bus until she got off because she needed some company. When we got to the last stop, she said, "You are coming home with me." She dropped the last passenger off, took me to the bus terminal, and gave me the keys to her car, telling me to bring the car around to pick her up. I thought she was joking about taking me home with her. She was going toward the shelter and got off at the exit. We went to the nearby grocery store and picked up something to cook that night. We had a nice dinner and a glass of wine. When we finished, I asked her, "Can I get something comfortable to sleep on? The couch?"

She said, "You are sleeping in the bed with me."

When I got in the room, she pushed me on the bed, took off my clothes, and put on some nice music. We had sex all night long. She wanted me to move in because I'd made some good loving to her. I stayed a couple of nights because she was cool and laid back.

I had to get back to the shelter and get ready to enter the master's program. I never let anything stop me from going to school. That was my main focus: to get my doctoral degree in a timely manner. I was talking to a guy in a restaurant, and he discussed how the world would be changing in the future with technology. I put the master's degree on hold and decided to go back to computer engineering school. I did a lot of researching before I made that decision. I went back over to the bus driver's house and spent the weekend with her.

While I was over at her house, I received a phone call from my mom about my cousin. She said, "You might want to seat down for this. Your cousin died a couple hours of ago."

I fell to my knees because we had grown up together since we were babies. The bus driver asked me what was wrong, and I told her, "My favorite cousin just died."

She said, "I'm going with you to support you." She took some time off of work, and we drove to my hometown to meet all of my family members. The entire family enjoyed talking to her about different things. A crisis was when most of family members got together and showed support for each other. We went to the funeral, and there were so many people that they had to open the church doors to let people sit outside. It was a nice funeral, but I was still hurt because my cousin was gone, and I didn't see him before he died. I didn't want to talk to a lot of people, so I went back to my room. I visited everybody before I left my hometown. My cousin had a good wife, and her name was Benita. She really took care of him until he died. They were married for a long time.

I always remembered the crazy things we did while growing up. We stole my uncle's cigarettes and went in the storage area and tried to smoke one. I pulled on it one time and almost choked to death. I never tried another cigarette from this day on. We used to fight over my grandmother's cheese biscuits every weekend. We used to walk to the store for my grandmother and pick up the groceries from the store. We would look after each other crossing the street. My cousin was a good-hearted person, and everyone loved him. He had made some bad decisions in life, but no one was perfect. I cried all the way back out of town.

We arrived back in town, and the bus driver dropped me off at the shelter. I thanked her for the support and said I would call her later; I needed some alone time right now. I went upstairs and thought about life, realizing I was blessed to still be alive. I could've been killed in the streets or in prison. When I got relaxed, Shontell called and asked me to come over. I jumped on the bus because no matter what, I still had a lot of feelings for her. I arrived at her house, and we talked for a minute. I told her, "I went my cousin's funeral because he'd just died." She acted like she didn't care. She was more concerned about where I had been the last few weeks. I told her I was about to move to another state to find a job and a new place. I left and didn't come back anymore.

I told Mr. Benny and his assistant I was about to move to another state, and I thanked them you for everything they had done for me. I packed everything and called Lexus, asking if she could she meet me at the restaurant so that I could see the boys before I moved. She brought them, and I gave them a hug and kiss and told them to call me. "I will come pick you up and spend some time with you."

I jumped on the next bus and went to another state. I arrived in this town lost. I caught a taxi to the nearest hotel, put my bags up, and went to the nearest restaurant because I hadn't eaten all day.

While at the restaurant I noticed an old man talking about how he needed to rent a place out that he had near a college. I approached him and said I would be interested in renting the place. He told me to meet him tomorrow and bring some money so that I could move in. I was so happy because most places would not let people with felonies rent; they checked everything, background and credit. It was blessing for me, and I thanked the Lord for the blessing.

I woke up the next morning with a smile on my face because I would have my own place with peace and quiet. I gave him the money, got the key, and went downtown to get everything else into the house. While I was downtown, I talked to this guy about some work. He told me a major company was hiring. I went over to the company and got the position. It was good because everything was in walking distance.

While I was moving everything in, I got a call from Jean asking me what I was doing that night. I told her I was moving into my new place. She agreed to come visit and help me decorate. When she arrived at the door, she was shining with her sunned, caramel chocolate skin. I decided to get some new furniture for my places. We rode around and found some good things. While we were out, I saw a good restaurant, so we grabbed some good food. We ate and talked about everything. We went back to my place, watched some movies, and then took it to the bedroom with some slow music. We made love all night long. The next morning she cooked breakfast as a thank-you for the beautiful night. When my furniture arrived, she had to go back to her job. I got the furniture in the house, and then Shontell called and said she was sorry, asking, "Could I come over now?"

I told her I had moved to another state. She wanted to come see me on the weekend. I agreed because like I said, she was still my baby. She said she was proud of me making a major move and getting my own place. I had a wonderful week with my job, and then I got ready to see Shontell. I saw an old friend from school named Marc. He showed me some love because he hadn't seen me in a long time. We exchanged numbers to stay in contact, and he would come by to check on me.

Shontell came that Friday looking really good—I wanted to take her clothes off right then. We decided to go downtown and check out some nice restaurants and wine-tasting galleries. We were having a ball with the nightlife. When she saw the horse and carriage, she stopped the man in the middle of the street. We jumped on it and rode around the whole city. The mood was just right. She was so excited and wanted to go back to the house to enjoy the rest of the evening. We got back, and as soon I got in the door, she put on some slow music, and took me to the bedroom, and undressed me, and made love to me like I'd never seen her do before. I was steaming and everything. She did it so well that I wanted to marry her right there, but I couldn't because I was still married to Lexus. She stayed with me the whole weekend, and we had a wonderful time together. She told me, "I really miss you a lot." I told her I would be coming to visit her more often. She had to get back to the home with the kids.

When she left the following Monday, I decided to go to the community college and apply for some side classes to get ready for computer engineering school.

While attending this school, I met a girl named Paula, and at the time she was taking early childhood courses. I noticed that every time I would come in the building, she watched me. We became really good friends. We had a couple of classes together, which let us become closer. We used to ride the same bus to and from classes. We became so close that she wanted to stop by my house. The first time she came to my house, she brought her daughter and mom. I really liked them because they were laid back. We decided to go out to eat and enjoy the new area. Her mom got comfortable with me because she would cook me some good turkey wings, and I would help out around the house when she needed me. Paula would help me with math because algebra was a challenge for me in school. We would go over problems until I got the concepts.

I decided to go home for the evening and take a walk downtown to get some food. I saw an old friend I grew up with during the nineties. We started talking about an old friend who had just moved to the area. He told me it was Bob, my best friend as a teenager. I got his number and gave him a call. I told Bob where I stayed, and he agreed to stop by and see me. We went to the store, got a couple of beers, and talked about the old days. I hadn't seen him in seven years. We decided to get back up the next day go out to the clubs in the area. We went to two places, and there were a lot of people. We met two girls who wanted to eat out after the club. We grabbed a bit of food, and then my homie dropped me off. We really enjoyed the night together.

I knew I had to get home because I remembered Paula was going to meet me in the morning to go to a couple of yard sales. She came around at eight in the morning. We ate breakfast first and then shopped around. We had fun enjoying each other throughout the morning. She dropped me off, and I went in the house to get some rest because I was tired from hanging out the following night.

While I was resting, Lexus called me out of the blue. She was on the phone crying about how she was in a bad situation with her boyfriend, and she had to get away really fast. My mom always told me, "Never worry about what people do to you; God will fight your battles. But always open your arms to help others." I couldn't stand to see my boys out there in a bad situation. I welcomed them into my home so that she could get her life back on track. I got my boys in school, and it was an excellent school.

Paula stopped by, and I explained the situation to her about how Lexus was having problems with her boyfriend, and I didn't want my kids outside. She was cool with it, but told me, "Don't forget about me, because I have feeling for you."

Everything was going smoothly until one day I was at class, and Lexus called me and said the kitchen was on fire. The fireman would not talk to me because I wasn't on the lease. I rushed to the house, hoping no one got hurt during the incident. I wondered how I would explain this situation to my landlord. He put a lot of trust in me without checking my background and my credit. I called him and explained the situation to him, and he was very understandable. The damage was pretty bad, so we had to move everything to a hotel. I thought to myself, *Is this really happening in my life?* We stayed in the hotel until we found another place. The agencies helped a lot; they were wonderful people and were very friendly. I made a major mistake and left a lot of my clothes in the house while we were at the hotel. The guys who were fixing the house left the front door open and took all of my suits and really good clothes. I explained this to the landlord, but he said he could do nothing about it.

Lexus found another house with more space. I was trying to figure out how she got the help when it was my house, but I didn't complain because my kids had to have somewhere to go. We moved in together, and I was still working down town. When we got settled in, I noticed she would start up again with the fights. I explained to her I was trying not to fight because I helped her out. She would start hanging out a lot, and I didn't care because I was focused on my school; we were basically going through the motions. I was spending more time with my boys, which was great for me.

I called my homie and let him know the situation, and he would come get me sometimes. He said he was having a major party next weekend, and he needed a bouncer for the door. I decided to take the job. I was going to school and would see Paula on a regular basis. I explained the situation to her, and she started crying. I had to hold her to comfort her.

I finished at the community college and was ready to transfer a lot of my credits to a technology school. I meet this white guy downtown when I got off of the bus, and he said he was on his way to the technology school. I caught a ride with him and got in. I put the master's program on hold until I finished the computer engineering program. I started going to school y and working at the same time. I wanted to learn as much I could about computers on the hardware side. This would be a two0year program, but I was used to the extended study time. I didn't know what to expect in the different classes. I went every day because I didn't want to forget anything. I overheard a lot guys say the course was hard, but that was a great challenge for me because getting my bachelor's wasn't easy.

I went home and told Lexus I was going to school to get a degree in computer engineering. She was proud of me and agreed that education was the key to success. It was tough, working a lot of hours and taking care of the boys' every need. I worked a lot of hours just in case I had get out again from her calling the police. I remember one Christmas I had enough to buy my kids some presents, but I wanted to buy them a lot. I got a call from my friend Marc, and he asked if I wanted to do some work over the holidays. It worked out perfectly because we had a good Christmas.

The following week Bob came and picked me up, and we went to the party he was having for the whole city. I was the bouncer and saw a lot of people from our hometown. I was searching people and noticed Lexus and some of her friends standing in line. Bob came up to me and said, "Lexus is here at the party." I said I saw her. We let her and friends in at no cost. The night was going smoothly until around 2:30 AM, when the club was about to close. I got on the dance floor and danced by myself. I was hoping Lexus would come out and dance, but she was too busy with her friends. A girl started dancing with me. Then Lexus came out on where and hit me in the back of the head. I don't why she would do that, because she was dancing with guys all night long. It didn't bother me because it was only a dance. I picked her up and took her outside. It was a crazy night. I didn't think about getting paid—I just wanted to get home. I apologized to everybody about the incident.

I went home and sat up for a while thinking about a lot of things between me and Lexus. While I was upstairs getting some sleep, she came in the house with rage and went off on me. I went back to sleep, and the next day she called the police and left. I went to get a room and got all of my tax information together before taking it to the tax people. It was good timing because I could get another place. I had faith in God the whole time because I knew if he could bring me out of the headaches, I was headed for something better. I didn't want see my kids go through all of the drama; I had it in my childhood, so I didn't want to let them grow up in it.

The next day I stepped in the tax office, and I noticed a beautiful woman sitting in a chair. I went straight to her and asked her, "Would you like to go on a date?" I was really just joking, but I was serious if she said yes. She did my taxes and got me a lot back due to school. We exchange numbers and then talked on a regular basis. Her name was Mecca. We went out on the town for bowling and a nice candle-lit dinner. I met her family and kids, who fell in love with me as soon as they saw me. I would go to a lot of basketball events with her when her sister would play.

I was still going to school and trying to get my degree, and I was so happy about the tax results. I bought my first car in that town We got real close, so I found a nice, quiet house close to downtown and on the good end of the street. It was perfect timing because my job was right down the street from the house. The rent was kind of high, but the landlord was really cool. We did a lot decoration to the house so that it would look nice. We had a lot of cookouts and invited a lot of friends over because we had a fenced yard.

I was outside one day and got some more bad news about one of my family members. The police nabbed my cousin Dopeman. I want to shut the whole cookout down. I tried to tell my cousin to come up to here and stay with me until he got himself together. I noticed every time I would come out of the house to go to work, this crackhead named Smooth would be standing on my porch. He would ask if I had any work for him. I gave him a job cutting the grass and keeping my yard looking good, because I worked a lot. He was a good guy, and I could trust him with anything. He reminded me of an old buddy back home that would stay on the grind. When I would go on vacation with the family, I would pay him to watch the house for me. The neighbors would say, "He watched your house like a hawk. If a raccoon came in the yard, he would run it off."

One thing I loved about Mecca was that she would hit the highway anytime, as long she had the money to travel. I was coming home from work one day, and Mecca said she had something to tell me: she was pregnant with my baby. We made sure she attended all of her doctor's appointments. I wanted to have my babyboy at my favorite college basketball team' hospital. We had a son, and I named him after my nephew, who'd died in a car accident. That was a beautiful time for me. I finally brought my baby boy home for the first time.

I had to really find a real good job to support my huge family. I continued to go to school to finish the computer engineering degree. I met some cool people at the technology school; I would hang with different guys who were trying to do the same thing I was doing. I knew that with this education I had a better shock of getting an average job; I was a felony and didn't have too many options to get a real good job. I started working a lot on my regular job. As I would worked more, I noticed Shontell and I were growing apart. She was a wonderful woman and a very understandable person; we have a good relationship every day. We had a major decision to make regarding our separation—a complete understanding about our baby. She finally moved out, and I decided to stay at a hotel because it was a little cheaper for me.

I stayed at the hotel for a while. Bob would come over to my room and make sure I was doing well. He asked me if I wanted to help him promote a party the following week. We put a lot of flyers together and passed them out to different stores. We went to our hometown to drop some of the flyers off for Bob's cousin Michele. We met her at a commercial store, and when we first saw each other, it was love at first sight. We exchanged numbers and became close over time. I loved being around her son and daughter. We used to get together when I would come down to my hometown. It was strange because I found out it was the daughter of the lady who would cook the best cheese biscuits in town. When I would come down, they also cooked the best food in town. I was hoping one day they would open a restaurant somewhere in town.

The following week we had the party, and it was a nice turnout. As the party was going, I noticed a lady that looked like friend of mine from my hometown. We introduced ourselves, and I told her my name was Malik. Her name was Stephanie. I thought to myself, *Are you serious? Another Stephanie!* We talked for a while and then exchanged numbers. We called each other on a regular basis. She invited me over to her house to look at a fence she was trying to put up in her backyard. I took a friend of mine with me to give her an estimate. She loved the price and said she'd let him know when she would be ready. We talked on the phone every day, and then she invited me over for dinner. We became really close in a couple of weeks. I let her meet my mom and my little boy, who was keeping my mom young because she had retired and needed the company. I got my mom's approval, and she wanted me to meet Stephanie's parents.

When her parents met me, they feel in love with me instantly because I was funny and motivated about education. They were both retired with bachelor's degrees; they were very serious about education. They were proud of me, but they wanted me to get more. Her dad was an old-school guy who was serious about his business. He encouraged me every day, saying, "The sky is the limit in life." They boosted my confidence. They also had the best family gatherings I had ever attended, and they made me feel very important in the family. I really enjoyed every moment around Stephanie and her family. We went to Myrtle Beach one summer, and her dad cooked the best gumbo in the area. We had a good time at the beach. When we arrived home, it was time to enjoy each other and her dog. Her mom was a great woman and would give me hints about marriage because Stephanie really liked me a lot. We had a great relationship, but we didn't take it far enough to get marry. We decided to go our separate ways, so I went back to what I knew best.

I continued to go to school and finally graduated from university with my associate's degree in computer engineering. It was a happy moment for me, and I was getting ready to focus on my master's degree. I got into my old school and took it slow because in the master's program, I had have to stay focused on a lot of writing. It was harder for me because my car had died, and I was back on the transit buses. I thanked God for the transit because without the transportation I would not have accomplished my goals. It was harder to accomplish a goal without any family support at every step of the way, but I just had to keep my eyes on the prize and keep faith in God that everything would be okay.

I had to move back in with my mom to get everything back on track. My company laid me off, and it was hard to find more work. I spent a lot of time with my son, because he was always there to comfort me and my mom. The assignments in the master's program got harder and harder. I was getting used to writing a lot of papers and was doing very well. When I wanted to take a break, the boys and I would go to the cafe to relax and enjoy the music. I would find my boys and continue to spend time with them every day. I noticed every time I saw them, they missed me a lot. They were getting bigger, so I wanted to be in their lives every step of the way. They were my pride and joy. I thanked God every day for being in their lives and for not being locked in prison. I knew as long as I stayed out of prison, I could make a way for them.

I was almost done with my master's degree, and I met this lovely lady named Latoya at the gas station. We exchanged numbers and went on a couple of dates. She turned me on to a place that had the best turkey wings in the area. I wanted to kiss her, but I knew we were just friends. We had a wonderful time getting to know each other. She was very independent woman. We decided to go to the beach one weekend to get away from everybody. We had a wonderful time enjoying the weather and walking the beach. I noticed she would give me a serious look, like she wanted me for life. We had a great time.

My phone rung on the way back from the beach and my agent called me and said there was a huge project going on in a new area. He asked me if I would be interested in going to the area. I didn't do any thinking about it. I got my car fixed, called my cousin, and asked him if I could stay with him until I found a place. He agreed, and so I put everything in my car and got to the area in no time.

When I arrived at the area, the city was looking nice. I had to report to Louis downtown to get my assignment. I met this guy who worked with Louis named Bryan, and he was also from out of town. He was a cool guy to talk to on the job site. I met my cousin and put all of my clothes away. I started the job and felt good working some of the guys. Everything was going smoothly.

One day Lexus called me and asked if I could keep the boys, because she needed a break. I agreed and told my cousin I had to find a place fast. "My boys are coming up here to stay with me.' I found a place close to downtown, and the landlord, Glen, and his wife were some of the best people I had ever met. I got everything together, and we moved into the place. While I was working for this company, I got an interview with the vice president of the organization. He liked my education and job experience. The interview went so well that he said he would call me for a second interview. A week later he emailed me back and asked me if I was still interested in the project manager position. I agreed, and he wanted me to take the assessment test. I passed it with flying colors. He said, "As soon as one tier opens up, you can start."

**God will make a way in your life to expose your dreams throughout your journey. We have to understand our covenant with Gods purpose and develop faith and trust.**

**Proverbs 3:13-19**

**Blessed are those who find wisdom,those who gain understanding,for she is more profitable than silver and yields better returns than gold. She is more precious than rubies;nothing you desire can compare with her. Long life is in her right hand.in her left hand are riches and honor.**

**Her ways are pleasant ways and all her paths are peace.**

**She is a tree of life to those who take hold of her;those who hold her fast will be blessed.**

# Conclusion

If I didn't have God or my master's degree, I wouldn't have had a shot with an interview with the vice president. Education is important if you have a dream to be something in life. I thought my felony would affect the VP calling me in, but I was happy to get a chance to interview with him. There is always hope—you can't give up your dreams. That's one thing I can always say: I talked to the vice president of a billion-dollar company to get a job. I thank my cousins for their help and will never forget their support.

I got my boys in some nice schools. My dream had come true: I had my boys to myself without her around. We had fun shopping and became connected again with a father and sons bond. It was a very excited moment in our life. They wanted to play football, so I showed them some of my moves from my days on the field. I continued to go to school and made sure they did well in school. We cooked together and cleaned the kitchen to make sure everything was in order. I told them every day about how a woman looks at a man who is in the kitchen cooking. "It is a positive thing when you are cooking for her."

A year later their mom came back and took them back. It hurt my feelings, but I thank God for letting me get the opportunity to be a real father on my own. I continue to go to school to purse my doctoral degree. It is wonderful because I keep my faith, and God has directed my path. I am striving for my doctoral degree, and I have only two years to go. This is my story so far, but it will continue.

Proverbs 3:24-30

When you lie down,you will not be afraid;when you lie down,your sleep will be sweet

Have no fear of sudden disaster or of the ruin that overtakes the wicked,for the lord will be at your side and will keep your foot from being snared.

Do not withhold good from those to whom it is due,when it is in your power to act.

Do not say to your neighbor,Come back tomorrow and ill give it to you when you already have it with you.

Do not plot harm against your neighbor who lives trustfully near you

Do not accuses anyone for no reason when they have done you no harm.

# About the Book

It all started in a small town on the east coast. I grew up in the projects. It was a challenge not to get involved in the negative activity going on around me, because I had dreams of being a professional baseball player. But there came a turning point in my life where I chose the wrong path. By not being focused on my goals, I took a liking to what I was seeing on the block. I saw all the nice cars and women the drug dealers had, and it quickly pulled me into the drug game. As time went on, I had a new goal, which was to become one of the biggest drug dealers there was and to have my own block. But all that came to an end when I drew my final straw with the law. Although I'd gotten in trouble many times before, I never would have thought a judge would've saw fit to give me a second chance…With a new lease on life, I decided to go to school and better myself. From that moment on, I have gained an associate's degree in applied science, an associate's degree in computer electrical electronic engineering, and a master's degree. It was a tough journey, but the motivation of that second chance kept me going to become the professional entrepreneur I am today.

# About the Author

Malik grew up in a small town. He is a motivated individual who encourages people to never give up on their dreams. This is his first book.

*"This written work has been transformed into film adaptation..."*

CPSIA information can be obtained
at www.ICGtesting.com
Printed in the USA
BVHW092157211221
624589BV00002B/369